# POSSESSING
# WHAT'S
# YOURS

# POSSESSING WHAT'S YOURS

MYLES SWEENEY

XULON PRESS

Xulon Press
2301 Lucien Way #415
Maitland, FL 32751
407.339.4217
www.xulonpress.com

# Table of Contents

# Introduction

f we are going to talk about possessing what is ours, then each of us must ask this question: What is mine?

Whether you notice or not, a lot of people in church talk about what is theirs. This promise is mine. That promise is mine. We talk about what is ours, we preach about what is ours, we sing about what is ours, but do we actually possess what is ours? Not very often. We don't know what it is like to live in many of the promises God has given us, even the ones we know very well.

How do we go from knowing the promises to experiencing the promises in our lives? The Bible gives us very clear and practical ways to possess what God has for us.

I am going to start with a very simple and very powerful verse of Scripture. 2 Corinthians 1:20 says, "For the promises of God are yes and amen to those who are in Christ Jesus." Do you believe that verse applies to you? If you are a born-again believer, then you need to believe it applies to you. If you are saved, then you are in Christ Jesus, and all of God's promises are now yours. They are yes, and they are amen, which means so be it.

That brings up a question really quickly. If all the promises of God are yes and amen for me and other believers, then how come so few of us are walking in those promises? How come so few of those promises are active in our lives?

We do not walk in God's promises because they do not automatically drop into our lives. We have to learn how to possess them. They are out there. They are like fruit, hanging on a tree and waiting for us to take hold. But there are certain things you and I must do to partake of the promises. We must learn how to possess the things God has given to us.

Because of that, the book of Joshua should be one of your favorite books of the Bible.

"The book of Joshua? Really? You mean the Old Testament book of Joshua?"

Yes! That's the one I'm talking about. That book should be one of your favorite books in the Bible because it is all about taking the Promised Land. It is a book about possessing the promises of God.

Romans 15:4 says, "For everything that was written in the past was written to teach us." The history of Israel, the Old Testament people of God, is a natural picture that speaks spiritual truths to us today (Hebrews 3–4). We need to learn these spiritual truths so we can repeat the Israelites' victories and avoid their mistakes.

The taking of the Promised Land recorded in the book of Joshua is a whole lot more than just a history lesson. It is a step-by-step manual on how to take hold of the promises of God. If we want to stop talking and singing about the promises of God and start possessing them, then our first step is to study the book of Joshua.

# Moses Is Dead

The story of the Israelites taking the Promised Land doesn't start in Joshua 1. It starts in the last chapter of the book that comes right before, Deuteronomy 34.

And Moses the servant of the Lord died there in Moab, as the Lord had said. He buried him in Moab, in the valley opposite Beth Peor, but to this day no one knows where his grave is. Moses was a hundred and twenty years old when he died, yet his eyes were not weak nor his strength gone. The Israelites grieved for Moses in the plains of Moab thirty days, until the time of weeping and mourning was over.

Now Joshua son of Nun was filled with the spirit of wisdom ...

...because he went to seminary.
No, I'm sorry. I misread that.

Now Joshua son of Nun was filled with the spirit of wisdom because Moses had laid his hands on him. (Deut. 34:5–9)

When the Word says Moses had "laid his hands" on Joshua, it was not just referring to some kind of ceremony. This was on-the-job training. Joshua stood beside Moses, worked alongside him, and learned from him.

> So the Israelites listened to him and did what the Lord had commanded Moses.

> Since then, no prophet has risen in Israel like Moses, whom the Lord knew face-to-face, who did all those signs and wonders the Lord sent him to do in Egypt—to Pharaoh and to all his officials and to his whole land. For no one has ever shown the mighty power or performed the awesome deeds that Moses did in the sight of all Israel. (Deut. 34:9–11)

That is the end of Deuteronomy 34. The very next verse in Scripture is Joshua 1:1: "After the death of Moses the servant of the LORD, it came to pass that the LORD spoke to Joshua the son of Nun, Moses' assistant, saying: 'Moses My servant is dead. Now therefore, arise, go over this Jordan, you and all this people, to the land which I am giving to them'" (1:1–2 New King James Version).

This is the first thing Israel had to learn to possess what was theirs: Moses is dead. The Israelites had to deal with the death of Moses. Until they did that, they were not going any farther. They were not going to be able to possess the Promised Land. They were not going to possess what was theirs.

Please listen to me, believers. The same thing is true for you and me. If we want to possess what God has for us, the first thing we must learn is this: Moses is dead.

What do I mean by that? Your Moses could be a number of different things. There is a different Moses for everyone. Your Moses could be a person. Your Moses could be something that happened to you in the past. Your Moses could be a time, or it could be a place. Your Moses could be a past failure or past success. Regardless of what your Moses is, you must come to a place where you can declare these three words: Moses is dead.

Moses is dead. Moses is dead.

I want that to ring in your ears all week.

Moses is dead.

To possess what is yours, you have to declare the death of whatever is holding you back. Maybe it's something horrible, terrible, and destructive. Maybe it's something wonderful that is making you want to do nothing but reminisce. Maybe it's a dumb decision. Maybe it's something that was done to you. Maybe it's an offense with someone or something. Whatever your Moses is, you are going to have to deal with it. You are going to have to look it square in the eye and say, "I'm declaring that you are dead. You are dead to me. You will have no hold on me anymore."

In Isaiah 43:18–19, God says to his people, "Forget the former things; do not dwell on the past. See, I am doing a new thing! Now it springs up; *do you not perceive it?*" (italics added). What a question. God is doing something wonderful, incredible, and new. He has it for you, right where you are. He wants it to burst forth. He wants it to happen in your life. Do you even see it? Do you perceive that it's there? Do you know it's about to happen? It's pregnant; it is about to give birth into your life.

What would cause you to miss this wonderful, incredible thing God is right on the edge of doing? Being hung up on the past. Unless you forget the past and put it behind you, you will miss the new thing God wants to do in your life. Unless you look at the past and say, "Moses is dead," you will miss it.

Are you making progress in life? A lot of people are not.

"You know, if I were just a better person—"

That has nothing to do with it.

"If I would just read my Bible another ten minutes every day—"

That would be good for you. I encourage you to do that, but it's probably not the issue.

"If I just—"

Listen. You are not making progress because you missed a step. In Philippians 3:13–14, Paul says, "Forgetting what is behind and straining toward what is ahead, I press on toward the goal." You are straining for what is ahead, but you missed the first step. Paul says step one is "forgetting what is behind." Skipping that step is like trying to run a marathon with a refrigerator on your back. You won't get very far, and it's not gonna be much fun.

The book of Deuteronomy ends with the death of Moses. The book of Joshua begins with this declaration: Moses is dead.

"Joshua."

"Yes, Lord? What is it?"

"Moses is dead."

That was not for informational purposes. The whole of Israel had been mourning Moses for thirty days already. Moses's death was not a revelation. This was not a newsflash. What was God saying to Joshua? Let me paraphrase God's words into East Texas vernacular for you: that which was ain't no more. It's gone. It's dead. It's over. I've got new things for you. There are promises for your life, but if you don't move beyond the past, you will never enter into them.

Your past may have been good. Your past may have been bad. What happened to you may have been wonderful. What happened to you may have been terrible. The bottom line is this: that which was ain't no more.

"Well, I just love to think about the 1960s in America. What an incredible time, you know?"

Can I tell you something? The 1960s are dead! They are gone, and they are not coming back. *American Graffiti*, *Happy Days*, The Fonz—they are dead. No matter how much you long for them and reminisce about them, they are not coming back. That time in American life is dead and gone.

"Well, I miss the old, week-long revival services at church."

I don't! Week-long revival services are dead. Hallelujah. They are gone. They are over. Feel free to try a week-long revival service at your church today. See how it goes. There was a time and a place for those. God used them for a season, but that season is over. The revivals were not all bad. Some of them were good and powerful. But here is the truth: no revival service took you into the promises of God for your life. Not one of them caused you to possess what is yours.

"I remember the good old days of this church, GCF Wharton, back when we only had fifty people. Oh, it was so wonderful. We were such a tight-knit group."

Let me tell you something. Fifty is dead.

"Well, fifty is too small. I liked it when we were right around one hundred fifty. There were enough people here, and it was just so—"

One hundred fifty is dead! We are not going back there again. It is always funny to me when people throw out numbers like that. They always pick a number that is over when they came in. One hundred fifty is wonderful as long as you are not number 151 walking in the door. We are not going back to that. That time is dead. It is over. It is done.

"I liked the way Brother So-and-So took up the weekly offering."

Brother So-and-So is dead. We don't take up weekly offerings around here. We are not going to pass the plate or emotionally manipulate people into giving.

"Well, my first husband—"

Your first husband is dead. That's not insensitive. It's just the truth. Your current husband doesn't want to hear about your old husband every thirty minutes. Come on. Your current marriage is not going to come into the promises God has for it if you spend all your time talking about your previous marriage.

In 1984, Sallie and I were living in Sacramento, California. I loved that place. It is one of the best cities I have ever lived in—absolutely beautiful. One day, after we had been there for almost three weeks, I walked outside and came running back in. "Sallie, Sallie! Come here. You are not gonna believe this."

We went outside and watched the one white puff cloud alone in the blue, blue sky because it was the first cloud we had seen since we arrived. It does not rain in Sacramento from mid-May through the first part of September, but it always stays lush and green because of the snow runoff from the mountains.

We lived an hour away from San Francisco, an hour and a half from Lake Tahoe, and forty-five minutes from the Napa Valley. There were several wonderful beaches not far away. In the spring, we were able to pick between snow skiing in the mountains or resting at the beach on any given Saturday.

We had a gorgeous home there. It had three different patios—one off the master bedroom, another off the kitchen, and one more off the dining room. It was beautiful, just blocks from the American River and a bike trail that ran beside it for thirty-something miles, dotted with parks.

I was working for American Express at the time and earning so much money it was obscene. I was not yet out of my twenties, making more money than I ever thought I would make in my life.

Life was good in 1984. Everything was wonderful, then God spoke. "Myles, I want you to resign, leave Sacramento, and move back to your hometown."

I seriously thought I was hearing from the devil. I knew God loved me, so I thought there was no way He would call me to do that.

I wish I could tell you some virtuous story about how I heard God speak, then resigned and moved the very next day. I cannot tell you that story because I sat on God's instructions for months. I was looking for confirmation that I was *not* hearing from God. Then Sallie started hearing the same thing, and I was thinking, *Oh no. This is not good. This is not right.*

Finally, the message got so clear we both knew to do anything other than this unthinkable thing would be to shake our fists in God's face like spoiled children and say, "We won't do what You're telling us to do." I could not live that way.

Against my better judgment and everything I wanted to do at that moment, I resigned from my job at American Express. They thought I was nuts. People from the home office called me to say, "What on earth are you doing?" When I told them that God was telling me to resign, they really thought I was nuts. They probably started thinking it wasn't such a bad thing that this crazy person was leaving on his own.

I took a 70 percent pay cut, and Sallie and I moved back to Wharton, Texas. We loaded up our possessions and drove back in July of 1984, just in time for a refresher course on South Texas humidity and mosquitoes. We moved into a dinky garage apartment. The whole time a part of me was thinking, *What on earth are we doing?*

This was before we had kids, thankfully. The apartment had a bathtub, and the owners had put a shower head in without putting tile or anything up on the wall. The paint and sheetrock were peeling off. The garage door on the apartment would not close, which meant the garage right below us was always exposed to the elements. That winter was an extremely cold one. We spent months enduring the icy air that came straight through the cracks in the floor. When my feet first hit the floor beside the bed in the mornings—oh man.

I remember those mornings. Sallie and I spent many of them sitting together quietly, having breakfast and starting the day. I never said it out loud, but I spent many of those mornings wondering about our decision. Did I just ruin our lives? Did I just eat too much pizza and think God spoke to me?

What if, during one of those mornings, Sallie had said, "Oh, I miss Sacramento. I miss our wonderful house there. Don't you miss the wonderful weather? Don't you wish we could get in our car and drive up to Lake Tahoe in an hour? Oh, I miss snow skiing."

What would have happened? I can tell you. We would have been in marriage counseling, signing up immediately. Can you fit us in this week?

But thank God, praise God, I don't have a wife like that. We both decided that Sacramento was wonderful. Sacramento was great. Sacramento was amazing. We built some amazing memories during our time there. But you know what? We also decided that Sacramento was over. It was fun and great, but that time was gone. God had something new for us, and we wanted it. We were not going to go back to Sacramento. Sacramento was dead.

We buried the past. If we had not done that, we would have never perceived the new thing God was springing up for us.

Deuteronomy 34:5–6 says that God Himself buried Moses. I really like that. From then until now, no one has ever found Moses's grave. Why? Because God understands people. Most of us who have been around for a while and learned a little bit about life understand people pretty well too. What would the Israelites have done? They probably would have dug up Moses, or at least made a big deal about his tomb. God didn't want that.

He buried Moses secretly so Israel would not be tempted to dig up the past—no exhuming the body, no annual pilgrimages to the shrine of Moses.

This is not just an Old Testament truth. Peter denied Christ three times. Three times he basically said, "I don't know the guy!" When Jesus saw Peter for the first time after His resurrection, what did He do? He asked Peter three times, "Do you love me?" (John 21:15–17). There is a lot in that picture, but here is the main thing: Jesus was telling Peter to bury the past. Three times Peter denied him; three times Peter loved him. It was done. It was over. It was in the past. Jesus wanted to do something new in Peter's life, but Peter had to stop camping on his mistake. If he did not stop dwelling on his failure, he would have missed the new thing Jesus wanted to do in him and through him.

What about you? How long are you going to hold on to that loss? How long are you going to camp in that place?

Maybe you went through a divorce. Maybe you went through a business failure. Maybe an awful, traumatic thing happened to you. Maybe you made a stupid decision you would give anything to go back and correct. Maybe you picked up an ugly offense.

You reacted to something in your past, and you continue to react to it. You see people through filters because of what you went through. You keep remembering. You keep rehearsing. You keep playing the movie over and over again. You keep sitting there like a victim, as if you have no choice but to let the movie play. All you have to do is get up, switch it off, and say, "Never again. I will not play that movie anymore. It is in the past. It is buried. It is dead. I am not digging it up, and I am not going to let the enemy dig it up." If it ever sneaks back and starts to play again, just cut it off before the previews are over. "Whoa, I don't want to watch that again."

It is over. It is done. If you don't bury it and walk away, you will never come into the new thing God has for you. You will miss it.

"Pastor Myles, you just don't understand what happened to me."

It is dead. Bury it.

"You don't know what he did to me."

Stop digging it up.

"I can't."

The Bible says you can do all things through Christ who strengthens you (Phil. 4:13). The Bible also says, "It is for freedom that Christ has set us free" (Gal. 5:1). Freedom to choose. Freedom to turn off the movie. Freedom to bash the projector.

Moses is dead.

If you are being held back, then you know what your Moses is. If you are replaying the movie over and over again, you don't need a fifteen-minute prayer time to figure this out. You already know. Your Moses was probably already popping up in your head from page two of this chapter. Look that thing square in the face and declare this again and again: Moses is dead. You are dead. You have no more hold on me.

Moses is dead. If we don't get that, then guess what? We do not hear the new words God wants to say to us. "Moses My servant is dead. *Now therefore, arise*" (Josh. 1:2 NKJV).

God's promises are hanging out there for you. Moses is dead. Now therefore, arise. Get up. Go take hold of them. Take hold of God's promises for you, for your marriage, for your family, for your life, for your career, for others, and for the Kingdom of God. Now therefore, arise!

Some of you do not have a "now therefore" because you have not yet buried Moses. That's why this is chapter one. It is not just a good place to start, it is where we *have to* start, just like the Israelites did.

Moses is dead.

# A Sense of Destiny

Moses is dead. We have turned the page; we are moving forward. What is the next step?

If you and I are going to possess what is ours—what God Himself wants us to have—then we must have a sense of destiny.

In Joshua 1:6, God speaks to Joshua and says, "Be strong and courageous, because you will lead these people to inherit the land I swore to their ancestors to give them." The generation of Israelites in the book of Joshua was the second generation to have the opportunity to possess God's promises. God originally promised the land to their parents. Forty years before, the first generation had been in the same place, standing on the threshold. They were so close, but they did not possess the Promised Land.

"Wait a minute. I thought God promised that land to them."

He did, but they didn't get it. Instead, they spent forty years in the wilderness dying off one by one. In Joshua 1:6, God was not so subtly reminding the new generation that the Promised Land had also been available to their parents, but they refused to possess it and suffered the consequences. He wanted to make sure the new generation had learned from that mistake.

Just as it was with them, so it is with us today. God's promises do not come to us automatically. If all we do is wait for them to come and jump all over us, we are going to be disappointed. We have to get up and go jump all over them. We have to learn how to possess God's promises because they are not ever going to possess us. That is not the way it works. They are not guaranteed. They are true. They are there, waiting for us to take them. But they are not automatic.

In Lamentations 1:9, God speaks about the first generation that did not possess what He had for them, saying, "She did not consider her destiny; Therefore her collapse was awesome" (NKJV). They did not discern their destiny. They did not believe in who God said they were. They did not believe they could do what God said they could do. Therefore, their fall was astounding. It was astonishing. It was awesome.

That is God's epitaph for the first generation. They came to the threshold of the promises, right to the brink. They could have had it all, but they did not get anything. Now, this will be written over them forever: "She did not consider her destiny; Therefore her collapse was awesome," (Lam. 1:9 NKJV).

Moses led that generation out of Egypt, through the Red Sea, and all the way to Kadesh Barnea at the entrance to the Promised Land. The people refused to go in, so God took them back into the wilderness and led them in circles. They cut big donuts in the desert for forty years. They wandered around pointlessly while all of the old generation died off. Then, right before they came back, God told Moses it was his time to die too.

At the end of Deuteronomy, Moses shares his last words with the people of Israel. He knew these people well—some would say too well. This was Moses's heart cry for the people of Israel, a plea from deep within him: "If only they were wise and would understand this and discern what their end [their destiny] will be!" (Deut. 32:29).

Oh, I so wish they were wise! I wish they would wake up! I wish they would smell the coffee! I wish they would believe who they are. I wish they would discern what God has for them and believe it is true. I wish they would believe their destiny could be theirs.

God did not promise that generation death in the wilderness, but that is exactly what they got. Why? Because they did not believe who God said they were. They did not believe they could do what God said they could do. They did not believe they could have what God said they could have.

They did not believe it. They did not see it. They had no sense of destiny.

Many Christians around the world are in the same place. Sad, but true. They do not believe they are who God says they are. They do not believe they can do what God says they can do. They do not believe they can possess what God says they can possess. They do not believe in the good future God has for them. They do not believe their lives can have much of an impact. These Christians are not going to possess what is theirs. They are going to miss so much of what God has for them, and they are going to miss so much of what God wants to do through them because they have no sense of destiny.

I first spoke the messages of this book in a series of sermons at Grace Community Fellowship in Wharton. In the middle of that series, I received a letter from a pastor in Bulgaria. It would have impacted me very powerfully anyway, but it had an extra effect on me because I had been working on the Possessing What's Yours messages for weeks and months beforehand.

It was a letter of gratitude from a pastor I had never met. He wanted to thank me for translating my Kingdom Families teachings about raising children to be mighty men and women of God into his language. Some other pastors in Bulgaria had shared a copy of the teachings with him. He and his wife had studied them, and it changed the way they thought about raising children. So many of the things taught in Kingdom Families were the exact opposite of what they had understood, especially considering their communist background. But they saw all the scriptural support for what I taught, and they began to implement the teachings into their family life.

This pastor thanked me profusely because he saw the 180-degree difference in his family. He recognized rapid, dramatic change for the better in himself, his wife, and his children. Excited about the teachings, he and his wife had started taking a large group of couples in their church through Kingdom Families. He wrote me the letter just to thank me for Kingdom Families and share about the tremendous fruit it was having in his family and his church.

When I read that letter, I sat down and wept. First, I thought it was amazing that God could do such great things through someone small like me. He is a master at that. God loves to take ordinary people and do extraordinary things through them. It blessed me to be reminded of that. Then I thought more about the contents of the letter, and I started thanking God. I am so glad that somehow, somewhere in my past I was able to lay hold of a sense of my destiny. I could never have guessed the details of what it was going to be, but at some point, I started believing God wanted me to do something big. It did not matter to me if it was going to be big in the world's eyes. I knew it was going to be big in God's eyes.

I never wanted to live life on a small level. I understood that from the world's viewpoint, my life could end up being a very simple, ordinary one. But I wanted to link my life with God's purposes and have an extraordinary impact for the Kingdom. Because I got that sense of destiny, I was able to listen when God asked me to spend more time studying Scripture. I was able to obey when He called me to spend more time in prayer and more time pressing into Him. I was able to repent when He showed me areas of my life that needed to be changed. God spoke to me and I listened because I knew He had much for me to do, and I was determined to do it all.

As I sat with that letter in my hand, another thought came to me. What if I had not picked up that sense of destiny? What if?

God, is there anything I have missed? Is there anything I have left on the table because I did not believe a part of who You called me to be or what You called me to do? Is there anything I have backed off from? Oh God, who out there is missing something because I did not respond to what You had for me?

I have a lot of favorite quotes, but I want to share with you one of my absolute favorites. This is top-five stuff right here. J.R. Miller once wrote, "Not many of us ...are living at our best. We linger in the lowlands because we are afraid to climb into the mountains.... We do not know what glory awaits us if only we had courage for the mountain climb, what blessing we would find—if only we would move to the uplands of God!"[1]

"Too low they build who build beneath the stars."[2] Come on, child of God, listen. If you are building beneath the stars, you are building too small. Think bigger. Think of what God can do. Yes, even through you. Stretch yourself to believe for more. Press into God and get a sense of purpose and destiny. Get an inkling that your life matters. You can be every single thing God destined you to be and do every single thing He called you to do. You can have maximum impact in your life.

On the other hand, if you do not catch on to a sense of destiny, it will be costly. There are numerous examples of this in Scripture. Time and again, people missed what God had for them simply because they did not have a sense of destiny.

I would like to take a look at just three examples from Scripture—three Old Testament kings who missed what God had for them.

## KING SAUL

> One day Jonathan son of Saul said to his young armor-bearer, "Come, let's go over to the Philistine outpost on the other side." But he did not tell his father.

> Saul was staying on the outskirts of Gibeah under a pomegranate tree in Migron. With him were about six hundred men, among whom was Ahijah, who was wearing an ephod. He was a son of Ichabod's brother Ahitub son of Phinehas, the son of Eli, the Lord's priest in Shiloh. No one was aware that Jonathan had left. (1 Sam. 14:1–3)

Jonathan, King Saul's son, was tired of waiting around. God had told Israel to go take down the Philistines, and in response, Saul had rallied the army. Everyone marched up to the Philistine camp, but then they stopped. Saul chose to sit and twiddle his thumbs. He and the army's commanders hung out with the priests, casting lots to see if God was still telling them to attack the Philistines.

After a while, Jonathan jumped up and basically said, "This is nuts! Didn't God already tell us we are supposed to take these guys on? Didn't he already tell us we would be victorious?" So Jonathan left with no one except his armor bearer, saying, "Come on, then; we will cross over toward them and let them see us.... If they say, 'Come up to us,' we will climb up, because that will be our sign that the Lord has given them into our hands" (1 Sam. 14:8–10).

If the Philistines called them up to fight, that would be the sign of sure victory from God. Stop and think about that. Isn't that the natural response anyone would expect?

Most Christians play games like, "God, if this is really what You are saying to me, tomorrow make the sky green, then turn it purple by lunch. That is how I will know You are speaking to me." Jonathan did the opposite. He picked something that was most likely to happen anyway as a sign, so God would have to make something crazy and unexpected happen only if He needed to stop them. In other words, he was saying, "God, if this is not Your will, then stop us. Otherwise, we are going for this thing."

Jonathan and his armor bearer walked up to the Philistine camp. "Hey, guys! You want to fight?" Jonathan said.

"Yeah, come on up," the Philistines answered.

That was it. The sign from God. Jonathan and his armor bearer went up and began to fight a whole garrison of Philistines, killing them right and left. The fighting made such a noise and tumult, the rest of the Israelites heard it and rushed into battle. God gave them an incredible victory that day.

That is a great story. There are a lot of wonderful truths and principles in there. It is great for teaching. But the question remains: What on God's green earth was Saul doing?

He was hanging out under a pomegranate tree, eating fruit and casting lots to see if God was still saying the same thing He said before they'd started marching. Apparently, Saul was not in a rush. He was still inquiring from the Lord whether or not they should go, even though God had already spoken.

Saul did not receive everything God had for him because he would not take a risk. If he had known who he was and what God had for him, he would have been acting like Jonathan. "Come on! Let's go get these guys! God, if you don't stop me, I'm going."

That was the attitude of the apostle Paul. Acts 16:7 says this of Paul and his traveling companions: "When they came to the border of Mysia, they tried to enter Bithynia, but the Spirit of Jesus would not allow them to." Oh, I like that attitude. So many Christians say, "If God says yes, I will do it." Why don't we flip that? Go for it unless God says no. It is just as easy for God to say no as it is for Him to say yes. Sometimes we wait for a yes as an excuse to sit around and do nothing because we are afraid to take a risk.

In the financial world, if you want a higher return on investment, you have to take on higher risk. The same thing is true for life. If you want a highly rewarding life, you must take risks. If you are to possess all of what God has for you, then you must learn to take risks. Sometimes you are going to have to just do it.

Peter is one of my favorite people in the Bible. I love Peter. The guy made so many mistakes. That is one of the reasons I love him. I can identify with making mistakes. Practically every time you turn the page, Peter is doing or saying something stupid. But you have to love the guy because he is always going for it. He does not want to sit around and talk. He wants to get up and do it!

One of my favorite stories of Peter is one that most Christians are familiar with. He and the other disciples are in a boat, traveling across a lake. A big storm comes up, and it is so bad they start worrying about drowning. Then they see someone walking on the water in the midst of the storm. Who is it? None other than Jesus Himself. He is out there, walking on the water as if it were dry ground.

Then here is Peter. I love Peter.

"Lord, if it's you, ...tell me to come to you on the water." "Come," he [Jesus] said. (Matt. 14:28–29)

We know the story. Peter gets out of the boat, walks on the water a little bit, and sinks. Can I tell you something about this moment? The crowd in the boat was not quiet.

"Well, I don't remember anything in Scripture about the other disciples talking in the boat."

It's not in there, but trust me. Especially in this kind of situation, the crowd is never quiet. Never. They always have something to say. "Peter, what are you doing?" "Whoa, whoa!" "Don't you climb over that, man." "You're an idiot!" "Get back in the boat." "Peter, stop! Don't!"

Then he sinks.

"I tried to tell him!" "You heard me tell him, right?" "Yeah, I knew it." "I told him not to." "Nutcase."

By the end of it, when he was bobbing in the water, they were probably laughing at him.

"Ha! Hey Peter! Watch out, here comes another wave!"

Yeah, yeah. Peter sinks. I get it! I already know. Almost every message I have heard on this passage throughout my Christian life has been about Peter sinking. Can I tell you something? Other than Jesus, only one other person in all of human history has walked on water—Peter. Not too shabby. For myself, I would rather drown headed for Jesus than drown in the safety and boredom of the boat.

"Well, my life is so boring."

Get out of the boat! If you do that, your life will not be boring for long. Come on! Take a risk in God. I am not saying you should do something stupid you thought up on your own. I am not saying you should act on some weird pizza dream you had the other night. I am saying you should do the things God Himself has told you to do. If His word for you is not clear, then get some good counsel. But when God says something clearly, go for it! Take a risk in God.

When you take a risk, one of the first things that will happen is a dramatic improvement in your prayer life. Rote, ritual, mumbo-jumbo, dull, tame prayers go out the window when you get out of the boat. Your prayers will get real fervent real quick. You will be pressing in. "Oh, God! Please meet me here! I need you!"

Science tells us when we take risks, our bodies produce endorphins. Those make you feel better and live longer. Just read about Caleb, Joshua's counterpart, in Joshua 14. The Bible tells us when he was eighty-five years old, his eye had not dimmed one bit (Joshua 14:11). He had not lost any of his vim, his vigor, or his fight. Eighty-five years old, and he was still going strong. What did he say at eighty-five? "Give me my mountain. God promised it to me. I want it."

Caleb had been around the wrong crowd—the first generation of deadbeat, unbelieving Israelites. They were the people of God, but they did not believe they could do what God said they could do. Being around them cost Caleb forty years, but he never lost his dream.

"Give me my mountain. I helped everybody else get theirs, now I want mine. I want it for me, and I want it for my descendants."

If you read Joshua 14 closely, you will notice something. Caleb helped every other tribe of Israel take their individual pieces of the Promised Land. That means he was the last one to get his piece. Yet the piece he wanted, Hebron, was one of the most gorgeous places in all of the Promised Land. Why was it still sitting there? Because Hebron is where the giants lived, the descendants of Anak.

"Wow, that piece looks amazing. Let's go take—never mind. It has giants. We'll take this other piece over here," the tribes of Israel said.

"I want it. It's mine," Caleb said.

Caleb went and got it. He did not want his retirement condo in Miami. He wanted his mountain. He wanted what God promised him, and he got it.

I believe the graveyard is the richest place in any town. Why? Because there lie buried all the promises never fulfilled. Most people leave this life without possessing everything that could have been theirs, and they take all those empty promises with them straight into the grave. When I think about that, something rises inside me and says, "Not me! I am not going to let that be written over my life. I will take risks because I have a sense of destiny and purpose."

As for Grace Ministries International, this is what we are looking for. This is what we are trying to build. We are going for a church full of risk takers. We want people who have a sense of purpose and destiny, who step out and do what God tells them to do. We want people who take risks in God. Most churches these days focus on increasing in number, but that has never been our goal. We want a church full of giant killers. That is our heartbeat.

"Well, I don't know how this is going to affect my marriage."

Go for it.

"Well, I'm not sure if my kids are going to—"

Go for it!

"Well, I don't know what this will do to my career."

Go ...for ...it!

If God says to do it, then do it. Cross the line. Step out into the water. Go kill some giants.

Saul did not possess what God had for him because he would not take a risk. He would not take a risk because he had no sense of destiny.

## KING ASA

The events of Asa's reign, from beginning to end, are written in the book of the kings of Judah and Israel. In the thirty-ninth year of his reign Asa was afflicted with a disease in his feet. Though his disease was severe, even in his illness he did not seek help from the

Lord, but only from the physicians. Then in the forty-first year of his reign Asa died and rested with his ancestors. (2 Chron. 16:11–13)

The message here is not antidoctor. The Scripture is not trying to say Asa should not have seen any doctors. That is not what God was saying in the Bible, and it is certainly not what I am saying in this book. This is not antidoctor. It is antiprayerlessness.

We should seek God in all things. King Asa did not get what God had for him because he was prayerless. Even in the middle of dire illness, he did not seek help from the Lord. By pointing that out, Scripture clearly implies if he had sought help from God, God would have healed him.

Why did Asa not seek God? Because he did not have a sense of destiny. He chose to say, "Oh, well. My time is up. If doctors cannot heal me, then I guess I just have to die." He could have said, "I have a destiny. I have a purpose. I am going to press into God and see if this is from Him or not. God, do You have another way for me?"

I know many people who, when faced with problems, talk to anybody and everybody except God. They spend all kinds of time talking to as many people as they can about their problems, but they never spend any time talking to God. I see people like this all the time.

Of course, we all need good counsel. There are many times and places where it is wise to seek input from other people. But many times we go to other people mainly because we want to complain. We want to back up the dump truck—*beep, beep, beep*—dump the load, then drive off. Maybe say as an afterthought, "Be sure to pray for me. That is why I shared all that stuff with you." Yeah, right.

Good counsel and teaching from other people are important. But if we only eat food from other people's tables, we are going to end up spiritually underdeveloped. We need to study and press in, seeking God and learning how to grow on our own.

When we face various situations in our lives, we should first and foremost seek the Lord. Our knee-jerk response to everything in life should be prayer and study of the Word, listening to hear what God has to say to us.

Paul instructed the believers to pray continually, or pray without ceasing (1 Thess. 5:17). Odds are he was practicing that himself. What does that mean? Paul was preoccupied with inviting God into every aspect of his life. So many Bible-believing Christians struggle with this. I see a lack of prayer everywhere, and I do not understand.

"Have you prayed about that?" I often ask.

"You know, it's just not that big of a deal," is the common response.

"What?"

"I just lost the keys to the house. God's too busy to mess with that."

"Really?"

"Oh yeah, He's kinda tied up with all the stuff going on in the Middle East right now. He doesn't have time for me."

Listen. It is not about the size of the problem. It is about you. God is interested because you are the apple of His eye. If it touches you, it touches Him.

God is our good Father. How would the greatest dad to walk planet Earth respond to every need of his children? If one of them came to ask him for help, he would be delighted simply because the child asked. That is our heavenly Father.

Be like Paul. Involve God in everything. Pray all the time about every single thing. Put it all before God because you know how much He loves you.

People who have been around me for a long time often laugh and joke about a specific thing I do. I pray for parking spots near the front door of where I am going. I really do. It does not matter if I am driving to a restaurant or Walmart or the mall. As I am pulling up to the destination, I am praying for a parking spot at the front, close to the door. Why? Because God loves me. I am the apple of His eye. Beyond that, I am redeeming my time, making it count to build the Kingdom. Why should I waste my time walking a mile to the front door? Let someone who is not building the Kingdom do that. I am faithful with my tithe. Why should I drive fifteen laps around the parking lot at two dollars a gallon? Let an unbeliever do that.

God loves me. When I think that way and pray for a parking spot, I do not think I am off at all. I think God just laughs. "There he goes again. He's praying for another parking spot. I love it."

God loves you. The size of the things you ask and pray about shows how much you believe He loves you. If you only bring big things to God, that should be a warning light. You might need to adjust what you believe about God and how He relates to you.

We should bring everything in our lives to God in prayer. Arthur Pink, a great writer and man of God, wrote that prayer ought to be like breathing in the life of a believer.[3]

Most Christians do not get what is theirs—what God Himself wants to give them—simply because they do not ask. James 4:2 says, "You do not have because you do not ask God." Uh oh. God wanted to give you something. God had something there for you, but you did not get it simply because you did not ask.

Contrast that with the words of Jesus as He spoke to His disciples: "Ask, and you will receive, that your joy may be full" (John 16:24). Put it before God. The worst thing that could happen is a simple no.

If you are going to err, err on the side of asking too much. That is a stretch for some people, but it is a good stretch. As for the Grace churches, we are going to err on the side of asking too much. First Church of Asking Too Much—we will take that label.

Asa missed what God had for him because he did not seek God. He did not seek God because he had no sense of destiny.

## KING JEHOASH

> Now Elisha had been suffering from the illness from which he died. Jehoash king of Israel went down to see him and wept over him. "My father! My father!" he cried. "The chariots and horsemen of Israel!"
>
> Elisha said, "Get a bow and some arrows," and he did so. "Take the bow in your hands," he said to the king of Israel. When he had taken it, Elisha put his hands on the king's hands.
>
> "Open the east window," he said, and he opened it. "Shoot!" Elisha said, and he shot. "The LORD's arrow of victory, the arrow of victory over Aram!" Elisha declared. "You will completely destroy the Arameans at Aphek."
>
> Then he said, "Take the arrows," and the king took them. Elisha told him, "Strike the ground." He struck it three times and stopped. The man of God was angry with him and said, "You should have struck the ground five or six times; then you would have defeated Aram and completely destroyed it. But now you will defeat it only three times." (2 Kings 13:14–19)

Jehoash did not possess what God had for him because of a lack of passion. He lacked passion because he had no sense of destiny.

God made an incredible offer to Jehoash through Elisha—total victory over Israel's main enemy in that day. The Arameans were pressing in on more than one side, attacking cities and advancing closer to the heart of the land of Israel. God offered Jehoash total victory, but Jehoash did not get a total victory. He missed his chance. Instead of seizing the moment, he was timid.

Listen to me: timidity is not a virtue. Timidity is not a godly characteristic at all. Jesus said we either need to get hot or get cold, otherwise, we will make Him gag (Rev. 3:15–16). That is the RMV translation—Revised Myles Version. But it is accurate to the meaning of what Jesus said. Get hot or get cold. Make a choice. Get off the fence. Get some passion. Get some drive. Stop bumping along through life. Stop living so stinking small.

God did not give you a spirit of timidity. If you have a spirit of timidity, you did not get it from God.

"Well, that's just my natural temperament that God gave—"

*Baloney!* Not true! Timidity will keep you from getting what God has for you. Do you think God would give you something that would cause you to miss what He has for you? No!

"I've always just been kind of shy and timid."

Oh, I don't doubt that. People pick this stuff up at very young ages. It is easy to become fearful of what other people think about you and start backing into the background. It is easy to become quiet and passive.

"That's just the way God made me."

*No!* That is a lie from the pit of hell. God did not give you a spirit of timidity. God gave you the Holy Spirit, and the Holy Spirit comes to make you bold. If you read through the book of Acts, you will see the same thing again and again and again: when the Holy Spirit came, the people of God became bold. It did not take the early church very long to catch on; they were savvy. They stopped praying for the situation at hand and started praying for more boldness. When they were attacked, when they were in trouble, when the Jewish leaders came against them, what did they do? They came together and prayed.

"God, please please, please save us! Waaa!"

Nope. They didn't pray like that.

"Come on, God! Fill us with more boldness. That's what we need."

God did not give you a spirit of timidity. He gave you a spirit of boldness from the Holy Spirit.

In Ephesians 5:18, Paul says, "Do not get drunk on wine, which leads to debauchery. Instead, be filled with the Spirit." That is a play on words. He was basically saying, "Don't get drunk on wine. Get drunk on the Holy Spirit."

Spend time with God. Spend time in the Word. Draw from the Holy Spirit. When you do these things, you are spiritually drinking and drinking and drinking from the Holy Spirit. If you hang around Him long enough and allow enough of Him to fill you, He will change your temperament. He will change your natural tendencies.

When God started the first Grace church in Wharton and called me to be the preacher, I said, "No way. I will do counseling. I've been doing that for years, and I am comfortable with it. I'll do Sunday school classes. As long as there aren't too many people and we are all sitting at a table, I'm good with that. I'll even speak at some men's events, but that's my limit."

That's not what God said. He told me I was going to be pastoring the church, preaching every Sunday.

I fought back. "No way! That's not me. I don't do that. I don't like that."

In the very beginning, I spent most of my Saturday nights at the church building, sitting on the steps and crying. I would go up there to practice my message, but almost every time I ended up just weeping and having my little pity party. "God, why are you making me do this? This is not who I am. I don't like standing up in front of people. I don't do public speaking. Come on, God. You know that about me. I will do anything for You, but You are making me do the one thing I don't want to do. I thought You loved me."

God changed me. Now I preach, and I love it.

"Well, if that's your natural temperament, then that must be the way God made you and the way you are just going to be."

*Baloney!*

"You just don't understand, Pastor Myles. I'm shy."

Keep drinking. You won't be shy for long.

Look at the history of the church through the ages. Read the stories of the great men and women of God. They were incredible Christians who did incredible things. Read their journals, the biographies written about them, and the accounts of people who were there. If you look at the way these men and women wrote and talked and prayed, something will probably strike you. Many times these believers said things that sound incredibly arrogant. They said outrageous things. They said bodacious things. They said things that seem to push the boundaries of heresy. But I don't think the problem is with those people or what they said. I think the problem is with us today. Christianity dropped its boldness a long time ago, and we have walked far away from it. The great, historical men and women of God understood something about what God likes and how God responds that we do not understand today.

Let me give you a great example: Smith Wigglesworth. What an incredible guy. I am not talking about ancient history here. Wigglesworth was alive in the early twentieth century. He was a plumber in England, then God called him to preach. When he spoke, he had such bad English that no one could understand what he was saying for the first two or three minutes of his message. The people who had not heard him before were always shocked. Then somewhere in there, the anointing kicked in and he would speak beautiful English and a powerful message.

Wigglesworth had a phenomenal speaking and healing ministry. All of his meetings drew massive crowds, and many people were healed from all kinds of physical issues. There are even stories of his calling up people with dentures, praying over them, and watching new teeth popping through their gums.

There are so many wonderful stories of the amazing things God did through this man. Here is one of my favorites, a true story recorded by multiple eyewitnesses. One time a boy came to Wigglesworth's house in the middle of the night and knocked on his door. He said, "My father just died. Will you please come and pray for him? My family and I believe God will bring him back to life."

Wigglesworth went to the family's house. They thanked him for coming and took him to the bedroom where the father's dead body lay on the bed. He had been dead for an hour or so.

As the story goes, Wigglesworth looked at the body for a moment, then grabbed it by the clothes, picked it up off the bed, backed up, and ran across the room with it. Boom! He threw the body against the wall, and it collapsed on the floor. The family was freaking out, but Wigglesworth just looked at the limp body for a moment, then walked over to it and did the same thing again. Boom! Against the wall even harder. All of the family members were crying at that point, telling one another, "This guy is a maniac!" "What on earth?" "Why did we bring him here?" Wigglesworth picked the man up a third time and ran across the room. Boom! Against the wall again. The body fell to the floor, but this time the dead man's head snapped up and his eyes popped open. He had come back to life.

Later in Wigglesworth's life, someone asked him how he was moved by the Spirit so quickly. This was his answer: "If the Spirit does not move me, I move the Spirit."[4] Wigglesworth wasn't moved by the Spirit's passion. His passion got the Spirit moving.

His answer sounds heretical, doesn't it? At the very least, it sounds arrogant. It was neither. Wigglesworth understood something about God that we do not. God responds to our passion for Him, our passion for His Kingdom, our passion to see lives touched by Him, and our passion to see Jesus's name glorified.

God will respond to a passionate man. God will respond to a passionate woman. Are you passionate?

I have been counseling individuals and couples for many, many years now. With most people I counsel, as soon as I can I ask them, "What are you passionate about?"

"Uh—"

And right there I have my answer. If you are passionate about something, it takes you all of about two seconds to tell someone what it is. For people who are passionate about more than one thing, it takes them just a half second more to start down the list.

If you have no passion, repent. Don't beat yourself up. Just repent. Say, "God, I see that I need to fix this. If I am going to possess what is mine, I need to have passion."

Jesus said, "Blessed are those who hunger and thirst for righteousness, for they will be filled" (Matt. 5:6). Are you hungry? The Greek word translated as "hunger" in that passage is a strong term. Jesus was not talking about your stomach growling a little bit for righteousness. He was not talking about wanting a righteousness snack. Jesus was talking about absolute starvation.

Most of us in America cannot come close to understanding what the term *starvation* means because very few of us have experienced anything close to it. We go five hours without eating and act like we are going to die.

If food falls off our plates and hits the floor, we don't eat it. That is not what true hunger looks like. A starving man does not say, "Is that spoon clean?" A starving man eats roadkill. He doesn't care.

Are you hungry for righteousness?

You have been making your way through the desert for days, not a drop of water anywhere. You would drink anything. You are dying for a drink.

Are you thirsty for righteousness?

When we come to that place, God answers. When our desire for righteousness and for Him is that strong, God responds.

When Jehoash struck the ground only three times, Elisha reacted. "The man of God [Elisha] was *angry* with him," (2 Kings 13:19). The Hebrew word there is a very strong term. Elisha was massively upset.

Looking at Elisha's life, his anger makes sense. We can understand why he got so ticked at young King Jehoash. Elisha had been a menial serving attendant to the great prophet Elijah for years. When Elijah knew his life was coming to a close, he turned to his servant, Elisha, and said, "You have been loyal. You have served me faithfully and excellently all these years. What can I do for you?"

Elisha looked Elijah straight in the eyes. "I want twice what you have" (2 Kings 2:9).

This was the guy dealing with Jehoash. Elisha knew what God was offering Jehoash. He knew what God was willing to do for the young king when he said, "Take the arrows.... Strike the ground" (2 Kings 13:18). Then he watched the king lightly tap the ground three times, probably not wanting to look weird or funny in front of people expecting him to be dignified and kingly. I imagine the old prophet just about came unglued, pulling his hair and yelling, "No! No! No! No! No! For want of a bit more passion, you could have had it all!"

Jehoash missed what God had for him because he lacked passion. He lacked passion because he had no sense of destiny.

Ephesians 2:10 says, "For we are God's handiwork, created in Christ Jesus to do good works, which God prepared in advance for us to do." The New Living Translation says it a little bit differently, "For we are God's *masterpiece*" (italics added).

Do you believe that? You are God's masterpiece. If any part of you has trouble with that, just go outside, look up to the sky, and shout to God, "I am your masterpiece!" Do that every day until it sinks in—homework assignment.

Ephesians 2:10 is a beautiful verse on the surface, but there is even deeper beauty and meaning hidden in the original Greek words. There are three key words in this verse.

The first word is translated as "handiwork" or "masterpiece." That is the Greek word *poiēma*, which means something very beautiful and expensive made out of fabric. For the ladies, think of the most extravagant bridal gown you have ever seen. Guys, we might have a little more trouble with this one. Maybe think of an incredibly expensive, tailor-made suit. You are God's *poiēma*.

The second word is translated as "prepared in advance" (Eph. 2:10). This is multiple words in English, but it comes from just one word in Greek: *proetoimazó*. That word means "measured beforehand." You are God's masterpiece, a beautiful garment, and He measured you beforehand.

Have you ever been to a tailor or a seamstress? If I walked into a tailor's shop and said, "I want an extravagant, magnificent, tailor-made suit," what is the first thing that tailor would do? He would get out a tape measure and start measuring me so that when I came back, the suit would fit me perfectly.

God measured you beforehand. Before you were born, God took out his measuring tape and measured you. When you do what God calls you to do, it fits you perfectly.

You can be a godly parent.

You can have a massive impact on your workplace.

You can change lives.

You can do whatever He called you to do. I promise it will fit every part of who you are perfectly because God measured you beforehand—*proetoimazó*.

The first time I ever visited the shop of a tailor or a seamstress was when Sallie had her bridal gown altered before our wedding. Before we walked in, I thought it was going to be a gorgeous place full of amazing clothes. It wasn't like that at all. It looked like chaos. It was a mess in there. The whole place was covered in articles of clothing that were half sewn at best. There were so many pieces and parts of so many different fabrics and garments lying around. It didn't seem like there was any rhyme or reason to any of it. Total chaos. I knew the place was supposed to produce beautiful things, but at that moment it didn't seem like the shop could produce anything that was not a complete mess.

That leads me to the third word, translated as "created." This is the Greek word *ktisthentes*. In the Septuagint, a very early Greek translation of the Old Testament, this is the word used in Genesis 1. When God first looked over the earth, it was formless. It was void. There was chaos. Then God spoke the word *ktisthentes* over it. Boom! Order. Structure. Life.

Sometimes my life looks like chaos. Nothing seems to fit. Nothing seems to work right. Nothing looks good on the surface. Even when it seems that way to me, God is speaking *ktisthentes* over it. God is speaking order and structure and pattern and plan and purpose and destiny. The steps of the righteous are ordered by the Lord, and the Lord delights in his way (Psalm 37:23).

You are God's masterpiece. God measured you in advance. The things He has called you to do fit you perfectly. And when you were born again, *ktisthentes* happened in your life. This is what it means to have a destiny in God.

Do you want to possess what is yours? Start believing in the destiny God has for you. Choose to act on anything that is holding you back from having a sense of destiny in your life. Press in and believe you are who God says you are and you can do everything He says you can do. Believe that you can be all He has called you to be for His honor, His praise, and His glory.

# Armed, Dangerous, and Chilled Out

We have been camped in Joshua 1 for the first few chapters of this book because God has a lot to say in just this one chapter of Scripture. Until now, I have zoomed in on specific verses and phrases. Now I want to zoom out and take a look at the big picture of Joshua 1, pulling from it things we need to learn to come into the fullness of our inheritance in God.

> After the death of Moses the servant of the LORD, the LORD said to Joshua son of Nun, Moses' aide: "Moses my servant is dead. Now then, you and all these people, get ready to cross the Jordan River into the land I am about to give to them—to the Israelites. I will give you every place where you set your foot, as I promised Moses. Your territory will extend from the desert to Lebanon, and from the great river, the Euphrates—all the Hittite country—to the Mediterranean Sea in the west. No one will be able to stand against you all the days of your life. As I was with Moses, so I will be with you; I will never leave you nor forsake you. Be strong and courageous, because you will lead these people to inherit the land I swore to their ancestors to give them.

"Be strong and very courageous. Be careful to obey all the law my servant Moses gave you; do not turn from it to the right or to the left, that you may be successful wherever you go. Keep this Book of the Law always on your lips; meditate on it day and night, so that you may be careful to do everything written in it. Then you will be prosperous and successful. Have I not commanded you? Be strong and courageous. Do not be afraid; do not be discouraged, for the LORD your God will be with you wherever you go."

So Joshua ordered the officers of the people: "Go through the camp and tell the people, 'Get your provisions ready. Three days from now you will cross the Jordan here to go in and take possession of the land the LORD your God is giving you for your own.'"

But to the Reubenites, the Gadites and the half-tribe of Manasseh, Joshua said, "Remember the command that Moses the servant of the LORD gave you after he said, 'The LORD your God will give you rest by giving you this land.' Your wives, your children and your livestock may stay in the land that Moses gave you east of the Jordan, but all your fighting men, ready for battle, must cross over ahead of your fellow Israelites. You are to help them until the LORD gives them rest, as he has done for you, and until they too have taken possession of the land the LORD your God is giving them. After that, you may go back and occupy your own land, which Moses the servant of the LORD gave you east of the Jordan toward the sunrise."

Then they answered Joshua, "Whatever you have commanded us we will do, and wherever you send us we will go. Just as we fully obeyed Moses, so we will obey you. Only may the LORD your God be with you as he was with Moses. Whoever rebels against your word and does not obey it, whatever you may command them, will be put to death. Only be strong and courageous!"

The first thing comes from Joshua 1:3, where God tells Joshua: "I will give you every place where you set your foot." That is quite a promise from God. But I have been walking with God long enough that I get suspicious when God says He is going to give me something.

"What are you saying, Myles? Are you saying you have begun to doubt God?"

Not at all. I am saying this: the longer I walk with God, the more I understand that His definition of the word *give* and my definition of it are very different. When God says, "I am going to give this to you," doesn't mean He is going to serve it up on a silver platter. It means the gift is yours, but you are going to have to take it.

"Well, that doesn't sound right."

It might not, but that is God's definition of giving. God told Israel, "Hey, this land is yours, but you are going to have to fight for it. I will be with you. I will assure you victory. But you cannot just lie around and do nothing."

It is no different for us today. When God promises us something, we have to go get it and fight for it. Yet sometimes we think we can kick back and take a nap. "I bet my promise will be here when I wake up." When it is not, what do we do? We kick back and take another nap, thinking one of these days it is just going to appear.

God does not give that way. What He has promised us is ours, but we will receive it only if we are willing to get up and go after it. That is how we possess our promises.

I know many Christians who are poor employees. They are lazy. They do half-baked work. They are insubordinate to their bosses. Then when they get fired or passed over for a promotion, they blame God.

"I thought God promised me an abundant life. I thought He was supposed to bless me."

He will bless you, but you have to get up and get after it. You have to do what God wants you to do and develop the character God wants you to develop. If you want to receive God's promises, you are going to have to move with Him.

I could give example after example from different areas of life. Many Christians struggle in their marriages. Their communication skills are practically nil. They bring their work problems home with them. They give no affection to their spouses, and I am talking about kitchen-level affection. They do nothing to make their spouses feel loved, respected, or trusted. Despite all of that, they are unwilling to read good books that could impact their marriages. They are unwilling to get counsel from anyone, professional or otherwise. Their marriages are rotten and going nowhere. They know it, and their spouses know it. What is on their minds? "Man, I thought God had something better for me. When I got saved, I thought all this stuff would get fixed."

It never just gets fixed. Strong, intimate marriages don't happen automatically. God promised it to you, but you have to get up and fight for it.

When I talk about taking our promises, I am not just talking about naming and claiming. Our efforts have to go beyond just blabbing and grabbing. Part of taking God's promises is developing the character He wants you to have. Part of receiving what He has for you is being humble and teachable, responding to what He says to you directly and through others. *If* God promised it to you, and *if* you are willing to believe for it, and *if* you are willing to fight for it, *then* God will give it to you. That is the way it works.

If you think God has more for you than what you are living now, you are probably right. I doubt anyone truly walks in the fullness of absolutely everything God has for them. But you know what? One of the reasons you have not received more of His promises is because you have not been willing to get up and take them. You cannot kick back and passively wait for God to serve up His promises to you.

That is the first thing we must learn from Joshua 1. To possess what is ours, we have to get up, go, and fight.

For the second thing, we are going to jump to Joshua 1:14, "Your wives, your children and your livestock may stay in the land that Moses gave you east of the Jordan, but all your fighting men, ready for battle, must cross over ahead of your fellow Israelites." The New Living Translation says it this way: "But your strong warriors, *fully armed*, must lead the other tribes across the Jordan to help them conquer their territory" (italics added).

God required all of Israel to be involved in the taking of the Promised Land, and he required them to go "fully armed."

This passage reminds me of the Navy SEALs. These guys are Navy special forces, trained to the nth degree. They are in peak physical condition. They are always prepared. Their missions are planned thoroughly and timed out to the millisecond.

Imagine a group of Navy SEALs slipping behind enemy lines at night to complete a mission. They travel almost soundlessly through dark waters in a black rubber boat, coming to a stop before they reach land. All of them slip silently into the cold water and swim ashore. Once every member of the team comes out of the water, the commander says, "All right, you guys got everything?"

One checks his gear. "Yep, I have my rifle."

Another looks down and says, "I have a grenade."

Another says, "I think I've got a knife. I'm ready."

No, that is not the way it would go at all. Navy SEALs would already know everything they had on them before they got in the boat. If the commander told them to check their gear, it would take them several moments because each one would have about fifteen different weapons and pieces of equipment on them. Navy SEALs go fully armed.

God wants us to go for His promises fully armed. You are not going to get your inheritance as a one-man band or a one-instrument musician. It doesn't happen that way.

"Well, I'm just into faith. I'm a faith man."

You had better bring more than just faith to the fight. Otherwise, you aren't going to get possess what's yours. How do I know? Because the Word says so. Hebrews 6:12 says we inherit God's promises "through faith and patience." In all your faith, you better get some patience. In all your faith, you better get some love. First Corinthians 13:2 says that you are nothing if you "have a faith that can move mountains, but do not have love." You cannot *just* have faith.

"I'm just into praise and worship. Boy, I love it. I dance. I shout. I'm just a worship kind of guy."

That is good. But if that is all you have, then you are not fully armed. With all of that worship, you had better get into prayer.

"Oh, that's what I'm into, Myles! I'm into prayer and intercession. I just intercede with passion."

Prayer is good. But if you *just* do that, then you are not fully armed.

I could go on, but you get my drift. If you want to possess the fullness of your inheritance, then you must operate in everything God has given you. He wants you to go fully armed.

Someone once asked Pete Rose, the famous professional baseball player, how he became so great at baseball and exceeded all his peers. This is how he answered: "It's real simple. Everybody else practiced what they were good at. I practiced what I wasn't good at." Pete Rose became a well-rounded player. He could do it all. In other words, he was fully armed.

"I'm just not that into worship."

You had better get into worship.

"I'm just not into prayer."

You had better get into prayer. You will not get everything God has for you until you become fully armed.

Joshua 1:14–15 also says, "You are to help [your fellow Israelites] until the Lord gives them rest."

That indicates we journey together, or we don't journey at all.

Does that mean we are responsible to bring everyone with us? No. Some of the brothers are going to lay down and quit, and there is nothing we can do about it. But for anyone who wants to go—anyone who is not getting offended or quitting but is pushing as hard as they can—we are going to journey together. We are all going to help one another reach the inheritance God has for each of us.

This is not a matter of getting your inheritance and then dropping out of the race. If you have reached what God has for you, then you have more time to help your brothers and sisters until they reach what God has for them.

Understand this: you are not going to get what is yours without other people. Here is the other side to that truth: other people are not going to get what is theirs without you. We are to go together. We are to help one another get to the destination. We are to journey together, or we are not going to journey at all.

We need to stop looking for John Wayne–style Christians. Oh, we like the idea of people like that. That is the way the church has operated for years. We idolize the idea of super-anointed Christians who come in and do it all for everybody else.

"I just can't seem to get victory in this area of my life. John, will you come fight my battle for me? Will you pray for me? Will you intercede for me and help me get victory? I can't do it because I'm just a little, regular, ordinary Christian."

Then John steps in.

"Oh, my goodness! How did you do it, John? Maybe three years from now my church will bring you in as a guest speaker again so I can get more of my inheritance."

That may have worked in past moves of God, but if we are going to get all of our inheritance today, we are going to have to take it together. We have to help one another get where God wants us to go. We have to lay our lives down for our brothers and sisters.

A young girl was seriously injured in a car accident. She had to be rushed to the hospital. By the time she got there, she had already lost a lot of blood. The doctor came to her little brother, who was sitting in the waiting room and said, "Son, your sister has lost a lot of blood. You are the best match we have right now. We need you to give blood to your sister so that she can live."

The boy sat stone-faced for a minute. His bottom lip began to quiver. Finally, he looked up at the doctor with watery eyes and said, "Okay, I will."

The doctor patted him on the back as they walked into the room where his sister lay unconscious, pale from loss of blood. The nurses put him on the bed next to his sister. He lay there, shaking just a little bit but trying to stay as still as he could. One of the nurses came over and put a needle into his arm. The boy watched his blood flow through a clear tube into the needle in his sister's arm. Minutes passed, and color came back into the girl's cheeks little by little.

After waiting for several minutes, the little boy looked up at the doctor and said, "Doctor, when am I going to die?"

The doctor did not tell him they only needed a little bit. The boy thought he was going to have to give all of his blood to his sister, and he was still willing to do it. That's a beautiful story. In the same way, we have to be willing to lay down our lives for our brothers and sisters in Christ.

The only reason you are where you are today, washed in the blood of Jesus and walking in the goodness of God, is because of other people who laid down their lives for you. First and foremost, Jesus laid down His life for you. But most of us are also where we are because other brothers and sisters in the Lord laid down their lives for us. As we go for everything God has for us, we have to learn how to lay down our lives for one another.

Imagine that your life is like $1 million. When God asks us to lay down our lives, most of us think He wants us to go to the bank, withdraw that $1 million in a big lump sum, load up wheelbarrows full of hundred-dollar bills, then take them to the church and dump them all on the altar. One big deal then this "laying down our lives" stuff is over and done with.

God says, "Nope. Take the wheelbarrows back. Change all those hundred-dollar bills for quarters. Then go out and give your life away one quarter at a time."

God calls us to lay down our lives bit by bit. We give our lives little by little so that others can come into the Kingdom and we can all receive what God has for us. Are you prepared to lay down your life like that?

This is true corporately as well as individually. When a Grace church plants a new campus, the original campus often temporarily or permanently loses core members with different gifts and areas of leadership. That is the members of the church corporately laying down themselves and their own desires so that God's purposes can be established in other places and other people can experience the fullness of what God has for them.

Let's look back at Joshua 1:9: "Have I not commanded you? Be strong and courageous. Do not be afraid; do not be discouraged, for the Lord your God will be with you wherever you go."

I have never commanded anybody to be strong and courageous. Have you?

"Joshua!"

"Yes, Lord?"

"I command you: be strong, and be courageous!"

The fact that God commanded Joshua and the people of Israel to be strong and courageous tells me two things. Number one, this was not optional. It was not optional for Joshua, and it was not optional for the people of Israel. God did not give Joshua and his people the Burger King treatment. He did not say they could have it their way.

God delights in us. When we make specific prayer requests, many times He answers those requests with what we asked for. But there are also times when God says, "This is the way it's going to be." In those times, you can pray, "Hold the pickles," all day long, your burger is still going to come with pickles. You are going to get it God's way, or you are not going to get it at all.

God did not visit Israel to take a vote on whether or not they wanted to be strong and courageous. He commanded them to be strong and courageous. God did not distribute a survey to see how long the people thought it would take to pack up and leave. They had been camped in the same place for weeks, possibly months, maybe even years. We do not know how long they had been in that one spot, but we do know it was a long time. They were all set up where they were, then God told them to pack everything up and leave in three days. There was no leeway. There was no negotiation. Three days to get up and get going.

Joshua 1:11 says, "Go through the camp and tell the people, 'Get your provisions ready.'" The New King James Version says, "Prepare provisions for yourselves." That was a new thing. For more than forty years, everybody had been walking out their front doors and collecting manna for food. For all that time, their clothes and shoes had not worn out. God did all that for them, but now He was saying, "New day. New time. Things ain't going to be like they used to be. Go and get provision for yourself. Get ready because we are moving on."

Some of the Israelites probably weren't too happy about the change. "I don't know if I like that. I mean, I kind of like this manna. It's a little bland, and it has gotten old, but you know what? It's kind of nice to just go out and pick it up in the morning. I think I'll just stay here."

"Fine. Stay here. But get this: there is no more manna coming," God said.

His commands were not optional.

The fact that God commanded Joshua and Israel to be strong and courageous also tells me they could be strong and courageous. If God commands it, you can do it. Always. God never commands us to do things we cannot do.

I would never go to one of my children and say, "Son, you're five years old now. I command you: solve this trigonometry problem." No good father with half of his mind would do such a thing. God wouldn't either. He is never going to command us to do anything we cannot do.

When God told Joshua to "be strong" (Josh. 1:9), He used the same word found in 1 Samuel 30:6 where it says David "found strength in the LORD his God." David and his mighty men had traveled away, then returned to find their home city, Ziklag, burned and all of their wives and children taken. It was a major disaster. The men, these mighty warriors, began to weep and wail. Their lives were in ruin; they lost everything.

It gets worse. Some of those men got together and said, "This all started because of David. Let's stone him." In the midst of all of this turmoil, David "found strength in the LORD," (1 Sam. 30:6). That literally means he made himself strong in the Lord. He sank his roots deep into God. He prayed in the Spirit. He got into the Word. He spent time in intimacy with the Lord, building relationship. These are things that God calls us to do, even commands us to do. He commands us to build ourselves up in Him. And if God commands it, then we can do it.

Joshua 1:9 goes on to say, "Do not be afraid; do not be discouraged." The Hebrew word translated as *discouraged* means "to break down under stress." God was saying, "Joshua, I command you: don't crack under pressure."

"How can you say that to me, God? I've got Jericho in front of me. I've got millions of people to lead. I've got a battle strategy to come up with. I've got a major headache. Man, I've got a lot of pressure on me. And that's just the battle stuff. I've also got to deal with all these administrative tasks, and I've got to divvy this land up between the tribes. There is just so much pressure!"

God was saying, "Don't crack, Joshua. Don't crack under the pressure."

"Why shouldn't I crack under pressure?"

God answers that question in the rest of the verse, "For the LORD your God will be with you wherever you go" (Josh. 1:9).

This is the God who created the universe. This is the God who put the stars in the sky and calls them all by name. This is the God who created everything on the earth. This is the God who is omniscient; He knows every single thing all at once. This is the God who has every single hair on every single head in the world numbered at any point in time. This is the God who is omnipotent; all power resides in Him. This is the God who is omnipresent; He cannot even be contained by the galaxies upon galaxies upon galaxies that make up the universe.

I, Yahweh, the Lord your God, am with you.

We talk about how God is with us, but most of us never really understand the true meaning of His presence with us. The infinite, awesome, powerful, creative God of the entire universe will be close beside you wherever you go. That changes things just a little bit, doesn't it? Suddenly the pressure doesn't feel quite so bad.

I remember one of the first times I was involved in a demonic deliverance. It was one of the times I was in prison—visiting, not a resident. I was doing a prison ministry. One day, I was ministering to a group of inmates when one of the guys visiting with me ran into the room, saying, "Come here, Myles! Quick!" I didn't know what was going on, but he grabbed my arm and pulled me into another room.

There was a man on the floor under the influence of a demon. His eyes were rolling into the back of his head, and all of his muscles were completely locked up. I said, "What happened?"

"I was just talking to him about the Lord, and all of sudden he just started doing this."

We began to minister to the man for more than an hour. During the process, he kept breaking through and becoming calm and responsive. Then we would speak to him about the Lord, and he would go back to a catatonic state.

This was a huge guy. His biceps were bigger than my thighs. One time, when he was in the worst of it, his eyes got milky and clouded over. He looked straight at me and said, "I'm gonna kill you." He had a deep voice already, but his voice went down several octaves. I was praying out loud as hard as I could, and when his voice went down, mine went straight up. Whoo boy. I had to clear my throat to keep from sounding like Mickey Mouse.

At that moment, part of me was thinking, "Lord, are you here? Are you with me now?"

Sometimes we ask that question even when we are not in dire circumstances. Are you with me now, God? In my daily life? During the workday? At home?

Don't give under the strain. Don't crack under pressure. The Lord your God is with you.

Most fathers learn a certain thing very early on. If you have a young child up on something high, like a tree or a swing set, you never stand close without keeping an eye on them. Why? Because the next thing you know, you will see a child flying at you out of the corner of your eye, and you had better be ready to catch. Either you stand far enough away where they know they cannot get to you, or you keep an eye on them because they will just throw themselves at you and expect to be caught. Why? "Daddy won't drop me."

What a beautiful picture of the faith and trust of a child toward a father. God wants to bring us to a place where we can do that with Him. Catch me, God! He wants us to trust Him and know He is always there.

A friend of mine had a daughter who, when she was very young, always responded to problems with the same phrase. It did not matter what had happened—a broken toy, an appliance not working, a scraped knee—she would always say, "It's okay. Daddy will fix it." When I heard that phrase for the first time, I went home and wrote it down in the front of my Bible.

It's okay. Daddy will fix it.

Do you want your inheritance? Then understand this: Daddy will fix it. You can go and be bold and be courageous because He is there with you. Don't feel Him? He's there. Whether you feel His presence or not, trust Him. He is there with you.

Don't crack under the pressure. Here is an even simpler translation of that phrase: chill out.

When there is a lot on my plate, sometimes I can be focused and intense. In those moments, I don't want to smile. I don't want to be joyful. I want to be intense, and I want to get things done. Sometimes people even ask me, "What's wrong with you, Myles?"

"Nothing's wrong with me. What do you mean?"

"You're not smiling like you usually are."

"I don't feel like smiling right now. You smile."

In those times, God often comes to me and says, "Hey! Myles! Chill out."

Sometimes I say, "No. You chill out. I'd rather wallow in my stress for a while. You just don't understand everything I have on my plate, God. Although You should; You put most of it on there."

Don't look at me like that. I know you say the same thing. It may not come out of your mouth, but the attitude is still there. "You chill out, God. I can't chill. You don't understand."

God says, "Chill out. It's okay. Daddy will fix it."

What are we talking about here? We are talking about trust.

Dr. James Truax is a godly man who has had a powerful impact on my life. One thing he has said to me frequently is: "Myles, there's got to be joy in the journey." He said that to me over and over, particularly in one season of my life. And it was as if God Himself was trying to speak to me through him. "Myles, there's got to be joy in the journey."

"I'm just intense right now," I'd say.

No, no! There has got to be joy in the journey. That is not just joy in arriving at the destination. There has got to be joy in the journey there. If there is no joy, something is wrong.

Psalm 94:19 says, "In the middle of all of my troubles, you roll me over with rollicking delight." Don't worry about it. It's okay. Daddy will fix it.

"Have I not commanded you? Be strong and courageous. Do not be afraid; do not be discouraged, for the Lord your God will be with you wherever you go" (Josh. 1:9). This was God's message for Israel, and it is God's message for us today. Be bold. Be courageous. Don't crack under the pressure. Chill out because I am with you.

God wants to grow us up. He wants us to have our inheritance in him even more than we will ever want to inherit it. He wants to get us there, and Joshua shows us the way. All we have to do is receive the truth and act on it so we can move forward.

# Be Strong and Courageous

In this chapter, I want to focus on one simple phrase: "Be strong and courageous," (Josh. 1:9).

Joshua hears this same thing seven different times. Moses is the first one to speak it to him. Twice he says, "Be strong and courageous," to Joshua in Deuteronomy 31 (vv. 6, 7). Then in the same chapter, God says the same thing to Joshua directly (v. 23). Later, in the first chapter of Joshua, God tells him three times, "Be strong and very courageous," (vv. 6, 7, 9). To wrap it all up, the people of Israel even tell Joshua, "Just as we fully obeyed Moses, so we will obey you.... Only be strong and courageous!" (Josh. 1:17–18).

Everybody was getting in on the action. "Hey! Joshua! Be strong and courageous."

When God says something one time, we should perk up our ears and listen. When He says the same thing twice, He means business. When He says the same thing seven times, do you get the idea that He is pretty serious about it?

This was massively important for Joshua to understand, and it is massively important for us to understand today. We can learn about possessing our inheritance from many different phrases and passages and truths in the book of Joshua, but this one phrase is worth camping on because God put it in His Word seven different times.

Be strong and courageous. If you are not strong and courageous, then you are not going to possess what is yours. You can talk about what is yours. You can preach about it. You can shout about it. You can whoop and holler about it. You can dance and sing about it. But you are not going to get it unless you are strong and courageous.

The word in that phrase translated as "strong" is the Hebrew word *chazaq*, which has three different meanings. First, it means "to fasten upon, take hold of, or get possession of." Do you want your inheritance? You are going to have to *chazaq* it. You are going to have to take hold of it. Fasten yourself upon it, and do not let go.

What has God told you about who you are and what He wants to do in your life? Fasten yourself onto that. Get possession of it. Take hold of it. Do not let the enemy shake you loose from what God has promised you. That goes for promises about you, promises about your family, promises about your children, promises about your career, and any other promises God has given you. Whatever they are, do not let go of them. Hold on to them like a bulldog.

Have you ever seen a bulldog that has a hold on something? It never lets go. One of my friends once had a bulldog, and he often used an old towel to play with the dog. When that bulldog sunk his teeth into the towel, the dog would not let go. It did not matter how much swinging and shaking and pulling happened. To possess what God has for us, we must be like that bulldog. We have to latch on to the promises and the callings God has given to us and refuse to let go. Otherwise, we are nothing but talk.

"Oh, God told me to do this, and God told me to do that."

Well, He told you that ten years ago. What have you been doing about it? You can say, "God told me to," until you go to the grave. Those words are meaningless until you take action. You will never possess what God has given you until you become strong. Lay hold of His promises. Fasten yourself upon them. Get possession of them, and don't let go.

The second meaning of *chazaq* is "to harden." In both the Bible and extrabiblical literature, this word can literally mean to harden the head or the heart.

Hardening the head or the heart can often be a negative thing. Exodus uses the word *chazaq* to describe what Pharaoh did when God spoke to him through Moses and said, "Let my people go" (Exod. 5:1). Pharaoh refused over and over again. He hardened his heart and mind, and that was a negative thing.

In Joshua, however, *chazaq* has a positive connotation. This is the only time I know of where the Bible speaks of being hardheaded as a good thing. God was commanding Joshua to harden his mind against any thoughts and lies from the enemy.

The enemy is sure to lie to you. "You'll never make it." "You'll never accomplish anything." "You'll never be anything." "Don't you remember what so-and-so said to you?" "Remember that time you did this?" "You are a failure, and you are always going to fail."

If you want to possess everything God has for you, you also need to harden your mind against the lies of the enemy. You must be strong against them.

You are also going to have to harden your heart against the temptations of this world. The missionary Jim Elliot once wrote, "He is no fool who gives what he cannot keep to gain that which he cannot lose."[5] The things of this world pass away. Your inheritance in Christ does not. Harden your heart against the things of the world.

In the Old Testament, Esau sold his birthright for a bowl of stew (Gen. 25:29–34). He gave up his inheritance for a mess of pottage. What a fool! When I first heard that Bible story, I was a young Christian just beginning to learn about following Jesus and just getting into the Word. I thought Esau was incredibly ignorant for trading his birthright for a little bit of food. I was thinking, "Man, I'm glad I'm not that dumb." Most people think that way about Esau and what he did.

The thing is, we spiritually do the same thing all the time. We give up the "rebirthright" God gave us when we became His in Christ to experience meaningless, passing pleasures. Are you going to sell out your birthright for a can of beer? Are you going to sell out your inheritance for a porno or an R-rated movie? Are you going to sell out your birthright so you can lie around, flip channels, and be a lazy slob?

We spiritually sell the inheritance God has for us in exchange for all kinds of things. We walk away from His promises because we have not hardened our hearts against the things of this world. The pleasures of the world are simple and fleeting. They are not worth trading your birthright. If we are going to possess what is ours, we need to harden our hearts against all the temptations this world has to offer.

The word *chazaq* also means "to be heavy." God was telling Joshua to be heavy. In other words, don't be a lightweight. Don't be a wimp. Don't be thrown around by every circumstance out there. Don't be blown along by the latest fad or doctrine. Be a heavyweight. Stand in there.

To receive our inheritance in the Lord, we have to be heavy. We have to stand in there.

The Word of God often compares us to trees. It uses that analogy over and over again. What makes a tree heavy? The fruit. When a tree bears fruit, the limbs get heavy. When the fruit of the Spirit comes forth in our lives, we become heavy. We are not tossed to and fro. We are not driven around by every wind of doctrine. We are not moved by circumstances. We are heavy. We are planted. We stay in there.

If you want your inheritance, you must be strong. You must fasten yourself on to what God has promised you. You must harden your mind to the lies of the enemy and harden your heart to the things of this world. You must be full of the fruit of the Spirit, not blown around by anything.

What about the second word in the phrase? Be strong *and courageous*.

The word translated as "courageous" is the Hebrew word *amets*. That word means "courage" and "boldness," but it also holds another meaning. *Amets* can mean "eagerness of the feet." In that word God was saying, "Be eager to walk in what I tell you to do. When I say go, get up and go."

Be strong and eager with your feet.

Just a few days after instructing Joshua to be strong and courageous, God tests him.

Early in the morning Joshua and all the Israelites set out from Shittim and went to the Jordan, where they camped before crossing over. After three days the officers went throughout the camp, giving orders to the people: "When you see the ark of the covenant of the LORD your God, and the Levitical priests carrying it, you are to move out from your positions and follow it. Then you will know which way to go, since you have never been this way before. But keep a distance of about two thousand cubits between you and the ark; do not go near it."

Joshua told the people, "Consecrate yourselves, for tomorrow the LORD will do amazing things among you."

Joshua said to the priests, "Take up the ark of the covenant and pass on ahead of the people." So they took it up and went ahead of them.

And the LORD said to Joshua, "Today I will begin to exalt you in the eyes of all Israel, so they may know that I am with you as I was with Moses. Tell the priests who carry the ark of the covenant: 'When you reach the edge of the Jordan's waters, go and stand in the river.'"

Joshua said to the Israelites, "Come here and listen to the words of the LORD your God. This is how you will know that the living God is among you and that he will certainly drive out before you the Canaanites, Hittites, Hivites, Perizzites, Girgashites, Amorites and Jebusites. See, the ark of the covenant of the LORD of all the earth will go into the Jordan ahead of you. Now then, choose twelve men from the tribes of Israel, one from each tribe. And as soon as the priests who carry the ark of the LORD—the LORD of all the earth—set foot in the Jordan, its waters flowing downstream will be cut off and stand up in a heap."

So when the people broke camp to cross the Jordan, the priests carrying the ark of the covenant went ahead of them. Now the Jordan is at flood stage all during harvest. Yet as soon as the priests who carried the ark reached the Jordan and their feet touched the water's edge, the water from upstream stopped flowing. It piled up in a heap a great distance away, at a town called Adam in the vicinity of Zarethan, while the water flowing down to the Sea of the Arabah (that is, the Dead Sea) was completely cut off. So the people crossed over opposite Jericho. The priests who carried the ark of the covenant of the LORD stopped in the middle of the Jordan and stood on dry ground, while all Israel passed by until the whole nation had completed the crossing on dry ground. (Josh. 3:1–17)

So often we read about works of God like this and think things like, "Oh man, that must have been awesome. It would have been amazing to be one of those priests carrying the ark."

I disagree. I don't think it would have been amazing at all. Sometimes we miss the truth of the Bible because we make the people in it larger than life. The Israelites were flesh and blood just like you and me. They had the same fears and the same struggles. "Was that God? Or was it not? I'm not sure. You know, I think it was. I believe so. I'm going to go ahead."

Here God tells the priests to load the ark of the covenant on their shoulders and march into the river at flood stage. During the flood stage, the Jordan would have been a raging torrent of a river, possibly more than a mile across. "Yeah, just get that thing on your shoulders and go across."

The priests probably did not respond with, "Oh, yeah! Great! Let's do this!" Their responses were probably more like this: "Oh, God. Is that water going to stop or not? Remember I can't swim, God. And remember, gold sinks. This thing is so heavy. Why can't Joshua go first? He's the one who got the word anyway. Why do I have to be the one to do this?"

Can you imagine how the priest at the front was feeling when they were four or five feet away from a river still running at full strength? "Come on. Come on! Part! Part!"

The situation did not change until their feet touched the water. Have you been there before? "Oh God, this circumstance looks so bad. It seems it's never going to end. I don't see how this is going to work out."

If you just stand there and stare at the situation, it does not matter what you do or how much you do it. Nothing is going to happen until you put your foot into the water. You can pray and confess God's Word and prophesy and speak in tongues all day long. Until you put your foot in, nothing is going to change. But when you step forward, God moves.

We cannot be circumstantially motivated. If we are going to possess what is ours, then we must be quick to move when God says to move. Our feet must be eager to obey God. Otherwise, we are not going to get what God has for us, and we will spend our lives on this side of the river.

It takes only one step, but it will almost always be the last step. So many Christians miss the move of God because they walk in faith and walk in faith and walk in faith, then they give up and back out right before God brings a mighty breakthrough or a tremendous victory. They do not take the last step. Because of that, they miss it all. Their testimony becomes, "God said, but it wasn't so." Not true. Just one more step. Don't give up too early. Put your foot into the water and see God move.

God does not ask us to work up strength and courage within ourselves simply because He said so. He did not command Joshua to be strong and courageous, then walk away, saying, "Figure it out." What did He say to Joshua? "Have I not commanded you? Be strong and courageous. Do not be afraid; do not be discouraged, *for the Lord your God will be with you wherever you go*" (Joshua 1:9 italics added).

God spoke the same thing through Moses one of the first times he told Joshua to be strong and courageous.

> Then Moses summoned Joshua and said to him in the presence of all Israel, "Be strong and courageous, for you must go with this people into the land that the LORD swore to their ancestors to give them, and you must divide it among them as their inheritance. The LORD himself goes before you and will be with you; he will never leave you nor forsake you. Do not be afraid; do not be discouraged." (Deut. 31:7–8)

How are we to be strong and courageous? By realizing God will always be with us. That is how we can have the strength and courage He calls us to have. That is how we *chazaq*. We can lay hold of God's promises because He is with us and will go before us. This truth is right there in one of His names—*Jehovah-Nissi*, the Lord our banner. He goes before us into battle as a victory banner.

In Joshua 3:4, God gives specific instructions to the people of Israel concerning the ark of the covenant, "But keep a distance of about two thousand cubits between you and the ark; do not go near it."

Why did they have to give it so much space? The ark was a physical symbol of God's power, glory, and brightness, and Scripture says it was where God chose to manifest His presence among the people. Why prevent everyone but the priests from going near it? If you read on through the Bible, you will find out. First Samuel 4–6 tells of a time when the Philistines captured the ark. Every place they tried to keep it in suffered horrible panic and disease and devastation. The Philistines passed it from city to city. "Hey, we've had this thing for long enough. Why don't you take it?" After playing hot potato for a while, they decided to get rid of the ark. They put it on an oxcart and sent it back toward Israel.

The ark rolled back into Israel's territory through a field right outside of Beth Shemesh. The men of that city were harvesting in the fields. They saw the ark and began to celebrate. In their joy, they forgot about the glory and power of the Lord upon the ark. Some of them opened it to look inside. As a result, over fifty thousand of them were killed.

Why did so many people die? Because of the awesome glory and power of the Lord upon the ark. That was the same awesome power and glory that went before the people of God as they crossed the Jordan River and took all of the land promised to them in battle after battle.

God Himself—His glory and power—goes before us today. He still leads us into battle.

In 1964, Malaysia and Indonesia were battling for control over the island Borneo. The British were on the side of Malaysia, helping them fight the war against the Indonesians. The British brought in a mercenary fighting force from Nepal called the Gurkhas. The Gurkhas were awesome fighters. Everyone feared them because they had no fear. They were bold and aggressive and full of warrior-fight attitude. Nobody wanted to go up against them. Almost every battle they fought in ended with victory for Malaysia.

Before one battle, the British strategists decided the best plan would be to parachute the Gurkhas in behind enemy lines. Since the Gurkhas had no experience or training in parachuting, the commanders decided to ask them whether or not they would be willing to do the jump. Considering the fearlessness of the Gurkhas, they were sure the answer would be yes.

They explained the plan to the Gurkha leaders, showing how flying them in and dropping them behind enemy lines would likely lead to tremendous victory. After hearing everything, the Gurkhas huddled in a conference for a while. Then they answered, "No. We are not going to do it."

The British commanders were shocked. They couldn't believe it. It was the first time the Gurkhas had shown fear or refused to do anything.

The next day, several representatives from the Gurkha force showed up at the British office. They came and said, "We've been rethinking your plan, and we will do it on three conditions. Number one, we don't want to be dropped near any rocky areas."

The British answered, "That's fine. The area we are planning to make the drop is all marshland. There won't be any rocks at all."

"Our second condition is that you fly the planes as slowly as possible."

The British said, "That's standard protocol. We always slow planes down to minimum speed for drops like this. What's your third request?"

"Our third condition is that the plane fly no more than one hundred feet off the ground."

This time the answer was different. "We can't do that. If you drop one hundred feet off the ground, there won't be enough time for the parachutes to deploy and stop your fall."

Then the Gurkhas said, "Oh, parachutes? We didn't realize you were talking about parachutes. We'll jump anytime."

That is the way we need to be. Be strong. Be courageous. Be bold. Jump out of planes flying one hundred feet off the ground without a parachute. God wants to put some of that attitude in us, His people. When He gives the word, let's do it.

God goes before us. What goes before God? Psalm 97 tells us.

The LORD reigns, let the earth be glad;
let the distant shores rejoice.
Clouds and thick darkness surround him;
righteousness and justice are the foundation of his throne.
Fire goes before him
and consumes his foes on every side.
His lightning lights up the world;
the earth sees and trembles.
The mountains melt like wax before the LORD,
before the LORD of all the earth.
The heavens proclaim his righteousness,
and all peoples see his glory.

A fire goes before Him. Lightning flashes go before Him. This picture appears in Scripture again and again. Psalm 18:14 says, "He shot his arrows and scattered the enemy, with great bolts of lightning he routed them." Psalm 29:7 says, "The voice of the LORD strikes with flashes of lightning." This is the God who goes before us.

Lightning heats the air around it to temperatures up to 45,000°F. No wonder the mountains melt like wax before the Lord. No wonder the enemy is consumed.

Be strong. Be courageous. Work it up? No, just remember and trust in the fact that God Himself goes before you. Fire and lightning and heat up to 45,000°F go before you. Your enemies do not stand a chance.

Ezekiel 21:9–10 says,

Son of man, prophesy and say, "This is what the LORD says:
  'A sword, a sword,
    sharpened and polished—
    sharpened for the slaughter,
    polished to flash like lightning!'"

The sword was made for striking like lightning. What did the sword represent? The prophecies of Ezekiel.

We already have the picture of God going before us with fire and lightning. In Ezekiel, the picture is different. This is not just about God. God was basically saying, "Ezekiel, I command you to prophesy. When say the words I say, they will be like lightning coming from your mouth."

When we say what God is saying, His power comes upon us. When we agree with God, spiritual lightning goes before us to melt our enemies and the mountains before us. When you come to faith and speak the words of God in faith, it's meltdown time, *The China Syndrome*–style.

At one point in His ministry, Jesus sent out seventy-two of His disciples to do His work. When they came back to Jesus, they were excited. Why?

The seventy-two returned with joy and said, "Lord, even the demons submit to us in your name."

[Jesus] replied, "I saw Satan fall like lightning from heaven." (Luke 10:17–18)

When Jesus's disciples spoke, demons left. If I had 45,000°F heat coming at me, I would leave too. When they spoke the words Jesus commanded them to speak and did the things He commanded them to do, it was just like lightning striking the devil. As we speak forth the words of God, it is like spiritual lightning.

Speak with boldness the words God gives you to speak. Don't mouse around when you pray for people. If your children feel sick, don't just pray sweet prayers full of Christianese. In every situation, speak the words of Scripture and the things God says to you with boldness.

Be strong. Be very courageous. Recognize and believe God Himself goes before you in all of His power and His glory.

# Gilgal

The story of Joshua and the Israelites continues in Joshua 5:1–12.

Now when all the Amorite kings west of the Jordan and all the Canaanite kings along the coast heard how the LORD had dried up the Jordan before the Israelites until they had crossed over, their hearts melted in fear and they no longer had the courage to face the Israelites.

At that time the LORD said to Joshua, "Make flint knives and circumcise the Israelites again." So Joshua made flint knives and circumcised the Israelites at Gibeath Haaraloth.

Now this is why he did so: All those who came out of Egypt—all the men of military age—died in the wilderness on the way after leaving Egypt. All the people that came out had been circumcised, but all the people born in the wilderness during the journey from Egypt had not. The Israelites had moved about in the wilderness forty years until all the men who were of military age when they left Egypt had died, since they had not obeyed the LORD. For the LORD had sworn to them that they would not see the land he had solemnly promised their ancestors to give us, a land flowing with milk and honey. So he raised up their sons in their place, and these were the ones Joshua circumcised. They were still uncircumcised because they had not been circumcised on the way. And after the whole nation had been circumcised, they remained where they were in camp until they were healed.

Then the LORD said to Joshua, "Today I have rolled away the reproach of Egypt from you." So the place has been called Gilgal to this day.

On the evening of the fourteenth day of the month, while camped at Gilgal on the plains of Jericho, the Israelites celebrated the Passover. The day after the Passover, that very day, they ate some of the produce of the land: unleavened bread and roasted grain. The manna stopped the day after they ate this food from the land; there was no longer any manna for the Israelites, but that year they ate the produce of Canaan.

If you are serious about possessing all God has for you, there are two things you need to draw from this passage of Joshua.

## LEARN TO BE FLEXIBLE

If you and I are going to possess what God has for us, we have to learn to be flexible.

Joshua 5:12 says, "The manna stopped the day after they ate this food from the land; there was no longer any manna for the Israelites, but that year they ate the produce of Canaan." The Israelites crossed the Jordan River, then everything changed. Back on the other side of the river, God had given them manna to eat. Every morning they woke up, went outside, and casually collected all the food they needed for the day.

Now they had crossed the Jordan River. They were beginning to possess their promises, but it was going to be a fight. Food was not going to come the way it used to. The Israelites had to learn to be flexible because everything was changing.

Back in Joshua 1, God gave them only three days to pack up and cross the Jordan River. Three days—we are crossing. Three days—we are doing this thing. Get yourselves ready, get your kids ready, get your dogs and cats ready, and get your parakeet ready because we are going across. There was no committee meeting. There was no discussion. There was no vote. They were going to do it, and they were going to do it right then.

Practically everything in their lives was changing. Their leadership was changing. Their source of food was changing. Their camping place was changing. Their daily routines were changing. Everything was changing, and in order for them to possess what was theirs, the people of Israel had to be flexible.

If there was ever a word for this day and time, "be flexible" is it. In case you haven't noticed, the pace of the world is changing. Things happen so quickly. It seems like everything moves faster and faster all the time. Someone once said, "Constant change is here to stay." They were very right. We live in a day of tremendous change.

Whether you think *change* is a happy word or a dirty word, if you want to be successful, then you must learn how to handle change. If you want to be successful in your marriage, in your family, in your career, or in any other area of life, you must learn to be flexible.

When people say they are flexible, that usually means they are willing to move with changes they choose for themselves. When they face changes they did not choose—change that stretches them, takes them outside their comfort zone, or conflicts with a belief—all of a sudden they don't want to be flexible at all. "No. Heck no. I don't want to change like that. That sounds uncomfortable."

Even when life is not going well, most of us still dislike it when change happens. Change threatens to take us into the unknown. We are not sure what is out there. Where I am might be bad, but where this change takes me might be worse. We simply do not like to leave what we know, even if we don't like it.

It is so important that we learn how to handle change. Even when it makes us uncomfortable, we have to open up our minds to change. A person's mind is a lot like a parachute; it will not do any good unless it opens.

The only way to reach your potential and possess all of your promises is to continually grow, and there is no growth without change. They go together, always. Keep growing, and keep changing.

One time after I spoke a message about change at a pastors' conference, one of the pastors came up to me and said, "Myles, I hear what you're saying, but the Bible says God is the same yesterday, today, and forever."

"You're right. That's true. But I have bad news for you: you are not God," I said.

God doesn't need to change, but you and I do. Even God, who is unchanging, is always on the move. It takes only a very casual reading of the Bible to see that fact clearly. God is always going somewhere. He is moving forward. Often we need to change so we can move with Him.

Does everything need to change all the time? No, what is sacred does not need to change. But we, as the Church, need to understand the difference between that which is sacred and that which is not. The Word of God and the message of the gospel are sacred, as is the truth of who God is, how He relates to us, and who we are in Him. Those things are immutable. We are never to tinker with them. But the packaging those things come in?

That is not sacred. We can change the packaging as much and as often as we need to. The message is sacred. The packaging is not.

The Church gets into so much trouble when it starts treating the packaging as sacred.

"This certain bell has to ring five times before we start the service."

That is not sacred. That is packaging. We should change the packaging often to fit the people we are trying to reach.

Several years ago I had a special meeting with several key leaders of the churches GMI works with in the formerly communist countries of Eastern Europe. They invited me to spend an evening with them doing a sort of Q&A session. They had a lot of questions, and they wanted to sit me down and hear my answers. I accepted the invitation with excitement. I thought it sounded like a lot of fun.

We sat together for quite a while. They fired questions at me, and I answered each one as best I could. We had some great discussions on many different subjects. It was a phenomenal evening. About midway through the meeting, one of the pastors asked about the services at Grace churches. He wanted to know how they were structured and what they were like. I described how we did church at GCF Wharton and the other Grace churches. As I explained, I watched these pastors begin to turn up their noses at me a little bit and glance at one another. I knew exactly what was going on. Finally, one of them spoke up, "Well, that's good if it works for you. We're just not into all that modern stuff. We don't like all those changes that some of the churches are making these days."

"I've got good news for you," I said. Eyebrows shot up. "No, I really do have good news for you. You don't have to change. You can stay right where you are."

A couple of them smiled. They were not expecting that answer, and they were happy about it. But I went on. "Can I just ask you one question, though?"

"Sure," they said.

"How's it going with your twentysomethings?"

They all hung their heads.

"That's what I thought. They're not there, are they?"

They shook their heads.

"How's it going with your thirtysomethings?"

"They're not there either. About mid-thirties and under, they're not in our churches," they said.

"When you lose a generation, it is so hard to reach the next one. It is one thing for thirtysomethings to reach twentysomethings. It is something else entirely for fiftysomethings to reach twentysomethings," I said.

You had better keep changing. You had better keep growing. You had better figure out what is sacred and what is not. The message is sacred. The packaging is not.

God is the same yesterday, today, and forever, but He is always on the move. This truth is obvious throughout Scripture, but one of the places we can see it most clearly is in the Old Testament when God took the Israelites through the wilderness.

God brought Israel out of Egypt and into the wilderness on the other side of the Red Sea. In that time, God led the Israelites in the form of a pillar of cloud during the day and a pillar of fire at night. They would camp when the pillar stopped moving. Then, when it started to move again, they would pack everything up and move with it.

Psalm 105:39 tells us the cloud was not just going before the people. The cloud was also over them. That makes perfect sense because these people were traveling through a desert. During the daytime, the temperatures would have been soaring. Then once night came, the temperatures would have plummeted to uncomfortably cold levels. This is where the cloud and the fire came in. During the day, God kept the Israelites cool by spreading His cloud over them and protecting them from the sun. Then when it got cold, He just turned on the burner and kept them toasty. He was protecting His people, watching over them.

That is a wonderful little setup. But each time the pillar moved, every single Israelite had a decision to make: pack up and move with God or stay where you are. They did not have to move with the pillar, but if they stayed, the protection of the pillar would no longer be over them. In all likelihood, anyone who did not move with the pillar either fried up or froze—another kind of frozen chosen.

Pardon my Christianese. "Frozen chosen" refers to stiff, rigid, and spiritually dead churches. I know a lot of people who have come out of churches like that. I am not talking about any specific denomination or type of church. I have been in ministry long enough to know the flag flying out front does not say anything about the level of spiritual life inside. You can walk in one church and experience incredible life, then go to another church of the same brand and find it dead as a doornail. I have seen Progressive Baptist churches with no evidence of progress whatsoever, and I have been in Charismatic churches that had me wondering, *Where's the charisma?* There are dead churches in every denomination.

Why does a church die? Very often it is because the people in it got the sacred and the nonsacred confused. Their unspoken motto is this: if the apostle Paul didn't do it, neither will we. Sounds biblical, but it is just plain dumb! Churches like this register as the closest thing to *Jurassic Park* I have ever seen. I am not even talking about how old and ancient everything is. I am saying there is almost always a lot of biting and devouring going on. Just sit in on a business meeting. If anyone suggests change, get ready for a T-rex to manifest, roaring and raging against it.

If you have experienced something like this, then you know exactly what I am talking about. If you have no idea what I am talking about, then you are blessed, my friend.

In the end, people still tell me, "Pastor Myles, I just don't like change."

Get in line. Virtually nobody in the world likes change. Change is uncomfortable. Change is unpleasant. Change takes us into the unknown. Change is hard. But when you have a genuine passion for God and a genuine passion to get everything He has for you, then the fire in your heart will melt the lead in your boots. With that passion in your heart, you are going to get up and move with God.

We have to grow. We have to change. Learn to be flexible.

## LEARN WHO YOU REALLY ARE

If you want to possess all God has for you, you are going to have to learn who you are. This truth comes from Joshua 5:1–2.

> Now when all the Amorite kings west of the Jordan and all the Canaanite kings along the coast heard how the LORD had dried up the Jordan before the Israelites until they had crossed over, their hearts melted in fear and they no longer had the courage to face the Israelites.

> At that time the LORD said to Joshua, "Make flint knives and circumcise the Israelites again."

This passage begins on a high note. The Israelites were saying, "Boy, this is a great day! Did you hear the good news? All of our enemies are shaking in their boots. Their hearts are melting in fear because of what God did for us. They don't even want to come out and fight us. Let's go get 'em! Come on! This land is ours for the taking!"

God said, "Hold on. Hold on. I like your zeal, but hold on for one second. There's one thing we need to do first."

"Sure, God. What is it?"

"I want you to go make some knives."

"Oh, good idea. We need some knives. Yeah, nice. That's good."

"Then I want you to take those knives."

"Yeah. Take the knives. We're ready, God."

"I want you to take those knives and use them to—"

"Say what? Come again? I don't think we heard you right, God. Something is wrong here. That can't be what you want us to do, and it definitely can't be what you want us to do right now!"

The Word says, "At that time" (5:2). At what time? At the time when all of Israel's enemies were afraid of them. At the time when the Promised Land was wide open, easy pickings. It was there for the taking. Yet God said, "No, no, no. You guys are not going anywhere until we deal with something first. Before you possess all I have for you, you must first come to a place where you understand who you are."

Please hear me on this. Before we experience the joy of conquest, we must first experience God's conquest of us.

That is what circumcision was all about. It was an Old Testament picture foreshadowing a New Testament reality—circumcision of the heart. Jesus Christ cut out the old person you used to be and gave you a new heart. You are a new person in Him.

At this moment, God commanded the whole of Israel to camp at a place called Gilgal. *Gilgal* means the "place of rolling" or the "place of rolling away." The Israelites gave it that name because it was there God told them, "I have rolled away the reproach of Egypt from you" (Josh. 5:9). He was saying that you are no longer who you were.

You are no longer who you were. You will never come into the fullness of what is yours until you settle that in your heart. You have changed. You are a new and different person. Second Corinthians 5:17 says, "Therefore, if anyone is in Christ, the new creation has come: The old has gone, the new is here!" You are no longer who you were. God has rolled that away.

Gilgal became the new home base for Israel. They stayed there not just for a week or a month but for several years. God wanted the Israelites to possess what He had for them, but for them to do that, they had to get the truth of who they were deep down inside of them.

Can you see what God was doing? Every single time they mentioned the name of their home, they reaffirmed what God was doing in their hearts.

"Where are you coming from?"

"Gilgal."

"Hey, where are you headed?"

"The place of God rolling away my past."

"Where are you hanging out now? Where do you live?"

"Gilgal. The place of God rolling away all I was before."

Because they camped there year after year, they had to keep speaking out the truth over and over and over. God wanted them to believe in their new identity.

If I hear a message that affects me or speaks to me, I wear that thing out. I have listened to some messages forty or fifty times.

"Myles, you're a nut."

No, I am a changed person. I just keep listening and keep listening until the truth gets deep within my heart. That is not easy to do. I can usually have something memorized before it gets into my heart.

My wife knows about a certain habit of mine very well. Our bathroom mirror almost always has some truth or quote that grabbed my attention tacked to it. I look at whatever is up there multiple times each day. It is always something God wants me to get deep down inside me. I just keep looking at it and keep looking at it until I get it.

Some notes stay on the mirror for a week. Some stay up there for months. I remember at least one thing that stayed on the mirror for about eight years. I tried to pull that one down one day about six or seven years into the process because I was tired of looking at it, but I immediately felt the Holy Spirit nudge me and say, "Uh-uh. Don't you touch that. You haven't got it yet. It's not really in you, and you need this. If you are going to get everything I have for you, then you need this right now."

God made Israel camp at Gilgal, leading them to declare the truth over and over again. What was He doing? He was trying to break off their slave mentality. He was trying to stop them from associating themselves with their past.

"We're nobodies. We're lowlife. We're at the bottom rung. We'll never be able to do this."

God was saying, "Who you were in Egypt is not who you are anymore! Stop and camp so that I can roll all that away from you. If you don't let Me roll that off of you and establish you in who you are today, you will never come into all the things I have for you."

God was rolling away more than just their slave mentality from Egypt. He was also rolling away the mentality of their parents, who wandered around the desert for forty years and died. He was telling them they were no longer restless, purposeless wanderers. They were now destiny-filled warriors.

You are not a purposeless wanderer. Even if you believe that is who you are, that is not who you are. If you are a child of God, born again through

Christ, then that is not who you are. It may have been who you were, but it is not who you are. You are a destiny-filled warrior. You are a person of purpose. You are a person of destiny.

Do you see yourself that way? Do you believe that about yourself? If I were in front of you right now, would you be able to look me in the eyes and say, "I am a person of destiny"? Not with a shrug and a "Yeah, I guess," but with confidence?

If you really believe you are full of destiny, something rises within you and makes you want to jump up and say, "Yes! That's me!" If you feel that way, then you are getting it. You have probably been at Gilgal for a while. The past has been rolled away. The old is gone. The new has come.

God knew if the Israelites were going to possess all He had for them, they had to see themselves differently. The same is true for us. God knows if you and I are going to possess all He has for us, we have to see ourselves differently. We must see ourselves correctly and truthfully. We must understand who we are through Christ and what he did for us.

Proverbs 23:7 says, "For as he thinks in his heart, so is he" (NKJV). Do you know what that means? Our actions will always be consistent with the way we see ourselves.

It is possible to rise above that level for a time. Maybe the Sunday morning service was especially good one week. Maybe worship was phenomenal. Maybe the preaching was good for a change. Maybe you had a great spiritual experience during the prayer time at the end. Those things can pump you up beyond the way you see yourself, but do you know what is always going to happen? After a short time—days, maybe weeks—you will drop back down and start acting according to the way you see yourself.

The opposite is also true. Maybe you made a detour in life. Maybe you made a few bad decisions, one after another. Things like that can cause you to drop below the level of the way you see yourself for a while, but pretty soon you will pop back up like a cork. Your actions will always be consistent with the way you see yourself.

Who do you really think you are? "For as he thinks in his heart, so is he" (Prov. 23:7 NKJV).

This is exactly like the phenomenon of the weekend retreat or the church camp. So many times people fall into the trap of thinking about special times and events as spiritual mountaintops and normal days of life as spiritual valleys. That is nonsense. That is nutty. Do you want to know the truth about the special-event situation? The "spiritual mountaintop" gets people all pumped up, but when they return to the routines of life, most of them drop right back down to the level of the way they see themselves. What about the ones who stay high up? What is the difference for them? Those who stay at the "spiritual mountaintop" level were not just affected in the moment. They had a change of belief. The level of what they believed about themselves rose, and the level of their actions rose with it.

If you want your actions to change and stay changed, then the real change has to happen in your heart. You have got to believe in who you really are.

You are probably tracking where I am going. If you have been a Christian for a while, odds are you have been taught some of the things the Word says about who we are in Christ. Whether or not you know the verses does not matter to me. Don't quote me the passages. I don't care. I used to quote those passages too, and that was long before I believed them about myself. It is easy to learn the verses and believe they are true. It is not so easy to get the verses deep in your heart and believe they are true for you. Those two are worlds apart. One of them will take you nowhere, and the other will take you into the Promised Land.

The GMI churches have been doing a program called *The Steps to Freedom in Christ* for many years. We did not create it, but it is an phenomenal program. We have seen incredible fruit from it. We first started doing the program because several professional Christian counselors recommended it to me. Each of them had a couple of good-hearted clients who wanted to change but just could not seem to break through. Then, independently of one another, the counselors tried walking through a new thing called *The Steps to Freedom in Christ* with those clients. Within a month, every counselor saw dramatic changes in the people they counseled, even in clients who had been struggling for years.

When they recommended this program to me, I thought, "Boy, I've got to find out about this." I went to a conference and received training on how to lead people through the program, then I came back and began to take church members through it. Since then, many other leaders have gone through the training and are leading others in the church through the program to this day (and doing a much better job of it than I ever did). If you go to a GMI church and you have not gone through the program, I strongly encourage you to do so.

*The Steps to Freedom in Christ* walks you through seven different areas from your past. It asks you to do a fierce spiritual inventory, then it leads you to spiritually deal with what you find in those areas of your life. Most people finish the process as a very different person from who they were at the beginning.

At the end of the booklet, after the last step, there is a brief section called "Maintaining Your Freedom." We always greatly emphasize this section; it is key to living daily life in the freedom gained through the program. The sad truth is many, even most, of the people who go through *The Steps to Freedom in Christ* do not do what the "Maintaining your Freedom" section recommends—to their own loss. Here is what it says in that section: "To maintain your freedom in Christ and grow as a disciple of Jesus in the grace of God, you must continue renewing your mind to the truth of God's word." Later it suggests believers "read and meditate on the truth of God's Word each day."[6]

What kind of truths should we meditate on daily? Let me give you just a few from the list the program provides:

**"I am God's child (John 1:12)."**[7]

"Oh yeah, I know that one. Next."

No! You might know it. You might have heard it once or twice before. You might have heard it over and over and over again throughout your entire life. But do you have it in your heart?

I am a child of God. I am His child. He is my dad. This incredible, amazing, and unbelievably loving God is my dad. That is who I am! I am not, as the old saying goes, a red-headed stepchild. I am dearly loved.

Do you believe that? You are not going to possess all God has for you until this truth is established in your heart.

"Well, I'm doing pretty good on that one."

You may be doing pretty good, but pretty good is a far cry from great. Pretty good is a far cry from all that God has for you. Settle these things in your heart. They will change you.

**"I am Christ's friend (John 15:15)."**[8]

Jesus chose me. That is the Greek word *eklektos*, which means Jesus sorted through all the options and picked me out from the rest. He selected me for a special purpose in life. I have a destiny, a calling, and a purpose for living. He picked me out for that. I am His chosen friend.

**"I have been justified (Romans 5:1)."**[9]

Do you see yourself that way?

Christians around the world have such anemic prayer lives. I speak from experience; my prayer life used to be the same way. It is such a widespread problem. I think this is partly because prayer is hard work. It is also partly because the enemy spiritually resists prayer. He understands how powerful it is. But I think it is mostly because so many Christians do not believe the truth from Romans 5:1. They say, "I don't think God would be very excited to see me right now. I didn't do too well this week. I slacked off over here, and I haven't been disciplined in this other area."

None of that affects how God sees you. You are holy and acceptable to Him.

I enter into prayer every day knowing God is excited to see me. He is waiting for me to talk to him. "When is Myles going to get here? I can't wait to spend time with him. Man, I love Myles."

That is true for you. Whether you believe it or not, it is true. That is the way God thinks and feels about you.

**"I am a saint, a holy one (Ephesians 1:1)."**[10]

"I'm just a sinner, saved by g—"

No, you are not! That is who you were. The Bible says that is no longer who you are. You are a saint. You are a holy one.

**"I cannot be separated from the love of God (Romans 8:35–39)."**[11]

"That sounds good, but I did—"

No!

"But—"

No buts! You cannot separate yourself from God's love. You absolutely cannot do it. No matter what you have done, where you have been, or how many times you have messed up, His love is pursuing you.

"Myles, I hear that. But let me just tell you, I have done so many awful things in my life. I have felt God's chastisement. He is coming down on me pretty hard."

Are you sure that is coming from God? Sometimes we bring things on ourselves and attribute them to God. But listen, even if you are feeling God's chastisement, it is just Him pursuing you because He loves you. He will not quit! He will not give up! If one thing does not work, He will try another. He is so in love with you. He will just keep pursuing you. You cannot outrun His love.

**"I am the salt of the earth and the light of the world (Matthew 5:13–14)."[12]**

"Well, I don't live that."

You do not live it because you do not believe it.

"Well, I need to start doing that."

No! That is the problem. You are trying to do instead of be. This is not outside in; it is inside out. Believe this. When you know this is who you are, you will live consistently with it. "For as he thinks in his heart, so is he" (NKJV).

I am salt. I am light. Once it gets in your heart, you will just start being salty and bright. You will become salt and light to everyone around you simply because you believe the truth about yourself.

You are salt and light. That is who you are. You cannot be anything other than who you believe you are.

**"I have been chosen by God to bear fruit (John 15:16)."**[13]

I can produce lots and lots of good fruit. That is who I am. If I did not produce good fruit, I would be living inconsistently with who I am. When I believe what the Bible says about me, fruit just starts popping up in my life. It is the fruit of the Spirit—love, joy, peace, patience, kindness, goodness, gentleness, and self-control (Gal. 5:22–23). My life is full of all of those things because it is simply who I am in Christ.

**"The good work God has begun in me will be perfected (Philippians 1:6)."**[14]

This is my favorite one. God started a work in me, and He is not going to quit. He is going to continue to perfect it, sometimes despite me. He will keep teaching and working in me because of who I am.

When we believe it, we live it. So many Christians are caught in the trap of doing, doing, doing in an attempt to change. It will not work that way. That is what the Pharisees tried to do—outside in. Change happens from the inside out.

Meditate on these truths. Camp on them, and get them deep within your heart. Believe they are true for you. Pick up the list every morning and every evening. Go through them. Highlight the ones that are important to you or the ones you have a problem with.

"Well, that sounds like a lot of work."

Do you want your promises or not? I know very many people who live in the abundance of God, produce great fruit, walk in incredible peace and joy, and do amazing things in the Kingdom. Every single one of them would tell you this is key to walking in that blessing.

As a pastor, I plead with you right now. I do not do that often. It is rare for me to plead. Please, please understand and believe the scriptural truths about who you are in Christ. These things will change your life.

To possess what God has for you, first you must learn to be flexible. Then you must learn who you really are.

# Jericho and Ai

Y ou have a destiny and a purpose and a calling in God. Do you want the full inheritance He promised you? Are you willing to do what it takes to possess it?

In this chapter, we are going to focus on the stories of Jericho and Ai in Joshua 6–7. The story starts at the beginning of Joshua 6.

> Now the gates of Jericho were securely barred because of the Israelites. No one went out and no one came in.

> Then the LORD said to Joshua, "See, I have delivered Jericho into your hands, along with its king and its fighting men. March around the city once with all the armed men. Do this for six days. Have seven priests carry trumpets of rams' horns in front of the ark. On the seventh day, march around the city seven times, with the priests blowing the trumpets. When you hear them sound a long blast on the trumpets, have the whole army give a loud shout; then the wall of the city will collapse and the army will go up, everyone straight in." ...

> When Joshua had spoken to the people, the seven priests carrying the seven trumpets before the LORD went forward, blowing their

trumpets, and the ark of the LORD's covenant followed them. The armed guard marched ahead of the priests who blew the trumpets, and the rear guard followed the ark. All this time the trumpets were sounding. But Joshua had commanded the army, "Do not give a war cry, do not raise your voices, do not say a word until the day I tell you to shout. Then shout!" So he had the ark of the LORD carried around the city, circling it once. Then the army returned to camp and spent the night there....

On the seventh day, they got up at daybreak and marched around the city seven times in the same manner, except that on that day they circled the city seven times. The seventh time around, when the priests sounded the trumpet blast, Joshua commanded the army, "Shout! For the LORD has given you the city! The city and all that is in it are to be devoted to the LORD. Only Rahab the prostitute and all who are with her in her house shall be spared, because she hid the spies we sent. But keep away from the devoted things, so that you will not bring about your own destruction by taking any of them. Otherwise you will make the camp of Israel liable to destruction and bring trouble on it. All the silver and gold and the articles of bronze and iron are sacred to the LORD and must go into his treasury," (Josh. 6:1–19).

I want to point out three things from Jericho before we move on to Ai. The first thing is this: God picked the hardest city first. Why did He do that? Why didn't He give Israel a warm-up? They had just spent forty years in the desert, so they had not fought anybody in a long time. Although there may have been some training going on, not one person in the whole nation had any combat experience. Then, right out of the gate, God led them against the biggest city of them all.

Why did God do that? I believe it was on purpose, and that He was making a point. There is no city too hard for God. You might even say it this way: there is no city too hard for destiny-filled people under the leadership and direction of God.

I go to pastors' conferences from time to time. During those events, I often hear things like this: "You have no idea what it's like in my city. It is so tough. If I were over there in Wharton, wonderful things would be happening in my church too."

It is so much easier to come to faith for somebody else's city, but God calls us to come to faith for the city we are in. There is no city too hard for God. There is no city too hard for destiny-filled, inheritance-possessing people.

The second thing we need to see from the story of Jericho is this: Joshua instructed the people, "Do not say a word." The plan was to march around the city like fools. This was an enormous city, fortified with huge, double-thick walls. The Israelites were going to march around it, carrying the ark and blowing horns. And not one of them was to say a word.

Why did Joshua give that instruction? Because he realized the carnal tendencies of man. He knew the people would be extremely prone to mumbling and grumbling and questioning and complaining and doubting. That is why the nation of Israel spent so much time in the desert; they could never come to faith. They murmured and complained about every little thing God said. Now God was asking them to do something more than a little crazy, and Joshua was saying, "Just shut up! Don't say a word. Don't open your mouths. If you do, I know you'll end up walking around saying, 'This is stupid. This is crazy. What is Joshua thinking?' I don't want all that unbelief out there! Just be quiet. Then when I tell you to, we're going to shout. Maybe by the seventh day you will come to faith."

We have to understand the power of our words. It is important to confess the words of God with our mouths. So many Christians spend more time confessing the words of the enemy than they do the words of God. The Israelites confessed the words of God when they shouted at the proper time, but before that they were quiet.

We have to be people who hear God and obey him without murmuring or complaining. If you have doubt, it is fine to be honest about your doubt in your own heart. But just because you have doubt does not mean you have to open your mouth. Do not spill your doubt on everyone around you.

This is the third thing we need to see in the story of Jericho: the sevens. Did you notice all of the sevens? Seven priests, seven trumpets, seven days marching, seven times around the city on the seventh day. Seven, seven, seven. What were the purpose and meaning there? What was God trying to say?

The number seven is the number of completion. It symbolically represents completeness and perfection throughout Scripture. For example, when Peter asked Jesus how many times we should forgive those who wrong us, Jesus said we should forgive seventy-seven times. Was He telling us to stop forgiving once someone has wronged us seventy-eight times? No, He was saying we should forgive ad infinitum; we should have perfect and complete forgiveness in all situations.

You can find the Hebrew word for *command* exactly seven times in the first chapter of Joshua, when the Israelites crossed the Jordan. God was symbolically telling Israel to walk in perfect and complete obedience. Partial obedience was not going to cut it. He wanted to bring them to perfect obedience.

With the sevens around Jericho, God was letting the Israelites know He was about to complete and perfect that which He had promised them. He had promised the land to their ancestors ages before, and the time for possession and fulfillment had come. He was going to completely and perfectly fulfill His promises right before their eyes.

I believe we—the churches of GMI, other churches around the world, and the corporate Church of Jesus Christ—are also living in a time when God is saying, "That which I promised you, I am now going to complete." Are there any promises or dreams you once had in your heart but have long since given up on? God is saying, "I'm bringing them back. I'm going to complete them. The time is now. It's time to take the land and get all of it."

Humanity is into starting things. God is into completing things. He is finishing and perfecting that which He began in you. He is going to bring all of His promises to perfection and completion. That goes for the things He promised to us, but it also goes for things God promised our forefathers.

"God, why did you choose me? I don't understand. I was so unworthy."

Maybe it had nothing to do with you. What if *you* are the fulfillment of a promise God gave your great-great-grandfather? Let that humble you. You might just be the answer to somebody else's prayer, whether that person was a natural relative or a spiritual forefather.

I believe the Grace church network is the result of other people's prayers. Our churches are the fulfillment of God's promises to people who cried tears for revival to come to Wharton and the Houston area and the whole of South Texas. We are the product of people who poured out their lives long ago. Our ministry is built on the work of those who went before us. Now God is doing a new thing through us, fulfilling His promises.

"Oh, God picked me because of my great gifts."

What if it had nothing to do with that? What if God raised you up and gave you purpose because decades ago someone prayed for the city you live in? God is going to completely fulfill His promises, and we are in the time when it is going to happen.

Those are the three things to see and learn from Jericho. We had to look at Jericho so we could get to Ai. The story of Ai starts in Joshua 7:1, "But the Israelites were unfaithful in regard to the devoted things; Achan son of Karmi, the son of Zimri, the son of Zerah, of the tribe of Judah, took some of them."

Achan took some of the spoils from the city of Jericho against the direct instruction of the Lord. God had said, "Jericho and everything in it is mine. Don't touch it. Nobody can have any of it because it is devoted to Me." But Achan took some of the spoils.

So the Lord's anger burned against Israel.

Now Joshua sent men from Jericho to Ai, which is near Beth Aven to the east of Bethel, and told them, "Go up and spy out the region." So the men went up and spied out Ai.

When they returned to Joshua, they said, "Not all the army will have to go up against Ai. Send two or three thousand men to take it and do not weary the whole army, for only a few people live there." So about three thousand went up; but they were routed by the men of Ai, who killed about thirty-six of them. They chased the Israelites from the city gate as far as the stone quarries and struck them down on the slopes. At this the hearts of the people melted in fear and became like water.

Then Joshua tore his clothes and fell facedown to the ground before the ark of the LORD, remaining there till evening. The elders of

Israel did the same, and sprinkled dust on their heads. And Joshua said, "Alas, Sovereign LORD, why did you ever bring this people across the Jordan to deliver us into the hands of the Amorites to destroy us? If only we had been content to stay on the other side of the Jordan! Pardon your servant, LORD. What can I say, now that Israel has been routed by its enemies? The Canaanites and the other people of the country will hear about this and they will surround us and wipe out our name from the earth. What then will you do for your own great name?"

The LORD said to Joshua, "Stand up! What are you doing down on your face? Israel has sinned; they have violated my covenant, which I commanded them to keep. They have taken some of the devoted things; they have stolen, they have lied, they have put them with their own possessions. That is why the Israelites cannot stand against their enemies," (Josh. 7:1–12).

There are several things here, but I have two main lessons I want to focus on from Ai.

By the time they reached Ai, the Israelites were pumped up. They walked up to the Jordan and watched the waters roll back. They walked up to the biggest city in Canaan and watched the walls fall right down. Then they walked up to Ai.

"Look at that tiny city. We don't need to send very many people there. Just send a few thousand. No big deal. Ai is insignificant. We don't need to pray about it, do we? Jericho was a big deal. We obviously needed to seek God for that one, but this one is so small. We don't need to seek God about Ai, right?"

I think I've made my point.

If we are going to possess our full inheritance, we must seek God for everything. The Word of God says we are overcomers, but we will never overcome on our own. "God, you've done a pretty good job so far. Thanks for that. But You can stop now. I got this. I can handle it now. Let me take over from here." Yeah, right.

We need God in the big things *and* the little things. We need to seek God for everything we do. We need to call out to Him. We need to press into Him. We need to do all things so that He is the one who leads us, goes before us, and gives us the power to achieve victory. We cannot do this on our own.

The defeat at Ai was not just caused by prayerlessness. It was also caused by robbery. The people stole from the spoils of Jericho. They took things that belonged to God.

Jericho was the tithe of the Promised Land. The book of Joshua tells the entire story of the people of Israel taking the Promised Land. They attacked city after city, capturing each one and taking the spoils. Guess how many cities they conquered—ten. We already know Jericho was the first city they conquered. Therefore, Jericho was the first tenth of the Promised Land, devoted to the Lord. Jericho was the firstfruits. That is why the spoils of Jericho were off-limits.

The situation boils down to this: Achan stole from the tithe. Then God told Joshua, "You will not be able to stand against your enemies until you get this right."

The defeat of Ai should teach us something. We need to learn to give God that which is His. Do you want the fullness of your inheritance? Then let me tell you something straight from the Bible. You will not get all that's yours until you get the tithe right.

When I first started writing this series on Joshua, I never in my wildest dreams imagined I would end up teaching on tithing. I had never heard anybody pull from Joshua to speak about the tithe, but when I opened up the Bible, there it was. I am not the least bit hesitant or ashamed to share this with you. I am not telling you this because I want anything from you. I am telling you this because I want something *for* you.

This was true for the Israelites, and it is true for us today: everything we have comes from the Lord. The first tenth of everything goes back to Him as a recognition of that fact. That first tenth is called the tithe.

The word *tithe* literally means "the tenth part," or 10 percent. Through the years, many Christians have come to me to say, "I don't tithe ten percent. I tithe five percent," or "I tithe two percent."

I tell all of them, "It's wonderful that you're giving something to God, but you're not tithing." The tithe means a tenth. You cannot tithe 5 percent or 2 percent because the tithe literally means 10 percent. When the Lord said the tithe belongs to Him, He was saying 10 percent of everything we have is His.

Some use this reasoning: "I made one hundred dollars this week. That brings the tithe to ...ten dollars. Wow. I mean, that's ten whole dollars. I'll tell you what I'll do. Let me go up and drop five dollars into the offering. I'll make an offering of five dollars."

That's not an offering. You cannot give an offering until after you have given the tithe. An offering is what you give out of your own money. The tithe is God's. If you gave five bucks out of one hundred, you are still a thief.

Another excuse I hear is this: "The tithe is under the Law, and I'm no longer under the Law because of Jesus."

Nope, that's not right. There is a lot of nonsense like that running around in the Church, but that statement is incorrect and unscriptural. Just look at Genesis 28:22. Jacob gave the tithe three centuries before the Law or Moses or Mount Sinai or the Ten Commandments. Where did he learn to do that? From his dad. Isaac taught him that. Where did Isaac learn to tithe? He learned it from Abraham, his dad. We can see Abraham tithing in Genesis 14:20. Where did Abraham learn to do that? From his dad. Where did his dad learn that? From his dad. We can go all the way back to Cain and Abel in Genesis 4, where Abel brought the first tenth of the increase from his livestock to God. Where did Abel learn to tithe? From his dad, Adam.

Tithing has nothing to do with the Law because it precedes the Law. Tithing has been around from the very beginning.

Here is where it gets even more interesting. If you go back and study ancient history, you will find that the Israelites were not the only people to tithe. The Egyptians tithed to their gods. That is a historical fact, proven by archaeologists. The Babylonians tithed. The Syrians tithed. I could go on because so many of the ancient civilizations tithed. Where did that come from? From the very beginning of humanity in the garden of Eden. God established tithing with the first man and woman ever, and their descendants took the custom with them when they scattered out across the earth. They ended up worshipping heathen gods, but they still understood and practiced the tithe. Tithing was not just a part of the law of Moses.

Proverbs 3:9 says, "Honor the LORD with your wealth, with the first-fruits of all your crops." It's the firstfruits, not the last fruits. We give to God the first tenth of our income. This is not, "Let's get to the end of the month and see what's left."

Can I tell you a dirty little secret? A lot of the people in the Church today do not tithe. Can I tell you why? Because they do not believe God. They do not trust God. They think, "I really need this money to pay my bills."

Do you trust God to supply your needs? If your excuse for not tithing is that you need the money, then apparently you do not trust God. Trust is a big issue for many people in the Church. But I think the bigger issue is this one little word: *materialism*. People tend to value their possessions and physical comfort more than they value the things of the spirit. Can I be honest with you? If your standard of living does not allow you to tithe, then you need to lower your standard of living.

"Well, I just don't have enough!"

Then change something. Get rid of something. Downgrade something. Do something. Your inheritance is at stake. If you want what God has for you, you have to get this right.

Leviticus 27:30 says, "A tithe of everything from the land, whether grain from the soil or fruit from the trees, belongs to the LORD; it is holy to the LORD." The tithe is holy to the Lord. Most Christians do not understand what that means. We take something very holy and sacred to God, and we treat it in a very unholy way.

Here is one example: some Christians decide whether or not they give the tithe based on whether or not they like the way things are going in their church.

The worship leader is playing the songs they like? They tithe. Too many slow songs? They quit tithing.

"I don't like the way they're doing cell groups."

"I don't like the way they changed that."

"How come they moved me to this group and not that one?"

"I am so upset at what the youth leaders said to my kid the other night."

Not one of these is a reason to withholding your tithe. Even legitimate complaints should have no bearing on whether or not you bring your tithe. The tithe is holy, but we make it unholy by the way we treat it.

Tithing is an act of worship. It is a practical expression of worship to God. When I use my time and energy and skills to earn money then walk into the church and give 10 percent of that money, I am giving praise to God. I am saying, "God, I praise You for the skills and abilities You put into me. I praise You because you gave me what I needed to produce this income. You gave me the strength and energy to do what I do, and You blessed me with the job I have. Thank you, God. I worship You for all of that."

When we tithe, we give ourselves. We put ourselves in the offering basket—our time, our energy, our effort. We offer ourselves in praise to God. Tithing is an act of worship.

The classic excuse is, "You preachers are always manipulating people for money. You're always harping on people, trying to get their money."

If you think that about me, then you just flat don't know me.

"Oh, I've seen pastors like you. You've got those nice cars and a nice house."

Yeah, I do. I am blessed. If you want me to feel ashamed for God's blessing on my life, you are wasting your time. Sallie and I have been faithfully tithing and giving offerings above the tithe since way back when we lived in a dinky efficiency apartment. Now we are living proof that tithing works, and I am not ashamed of that.

God has blessed us not only financially but also with a wonderful marriage. I would not trade my marriage for any other marriage in the world. That is honest and straight and true from my own heart. I would not trade my kids and the relationships I have with them for anybody else's.

God has blessed me in so many ways. He blessed me with an understanding of His Word. The chapters and truths of this book are an example of how He opens up His Word to me.

I believe all of the blessings I have experienced in my life are tied, in part, to the fact that I tithe faithfully. The blessing does not come solely because of the tithe. I have to walk in obedience to the Lord in other ways. But tithing is a big part of it.

When I first started pastoring GCF Wharton, I did so for the first several years without a salary. After a few years, the elders insisted I start taking a reasonable salary for what I was doing. They did not give me a choice, and they did not let me argue. But I have never been motivated by money. For the vast majority of my time as a pastor, I have also run my own business on the side. I have lost more than twice what I made at the church just because of the time and energy I put into the church instead of in my own business. Why tell you that? Because of how many times I have heard accusations like this one: "You're just fleecing the sheep." I want you to know I ain't got none of your wool in my house.

I write this for your benefit. I want you to be blessed as I have been blessed. In Malachi 3, God invites us to test Him and prove Him in His word that the tithe will bring blessing. I have tried Him, and He has proven Himself to me over and over. I want you to experience that same blessing.

There is one other reason I am writing this message. I want you to know the truth about tithing because I want the corporate Church to be blessed.

When Achan took some of God's money and put it into his bank account, the whole nation suffered. In Joshua 7:11–13, God says, "Israel has sinned; they have violated my covenant, which I commanded them to keep. They have taken some of the devoted things; they have stolen, they have lied, they have put them with their own possessions. That is why the Israelites cannot stand against their enemies.... You cannot stand against your enemies until you remove them."

God did not curse the Israelites. He did not say, "You took some of what was mine, so I cursed you." He basically said, "You guys broke covenant with Me. When you did that, you left My umbrella of protection and got whipped. You cannot stand against your enemies outside of Me, but you are the ones who walked away. I am just letting you know what you did. I hope you will repent and get back under My protection."

God was not beating up on them for taking His stuff. Israel broke the covenant with Him. They walked out on Him; He did not walk out on them. God was not taking them to the woodshed. They went there of their own accord and handed the stick to their enemy. God had nothing to do with it. He was back in the house saying, "Come on! Come back in!"

Until they got the tithe right, they could not stand against their enemies.

That truth scares me. It makes me think of all the believers today who do not faithfully tithe. How does that affect the whole of the Church? In light of Scripture, I think that is a good question. So many Christians in America have much of God's money in their bank accounts. I wonder how much that keeps the body of Christ from doing what God has called us to do in this nation.

Christians everywhere say things like, "Oh God, we want revival! We're crying out for you to move!"

God is saying, "Get this right. Get the tithe right. You are not going to be able to stand against your enemies unless you get this right."

Is that why our spiritual warfare is so anemic? Is that why such a small percentage of people receive healing from our prayers? Is that why our evangelism does not seem to touch as many lives as we think it could and should?

If this is hard to hear, I understand. I just want to expose the truth and give you a chance to walk away from deception. I want light to shine in your heart, and I want you to be free to receive all that God has for you. I want you to possess your full inheritance. I want God's plans and desires for you to fully and completely take place, and I know if you do not get this right, there will be some hindrances.

In Malachi 3:8–10, God speaks clearly about tithing and the consequences of both faithfully tithing and withholding the tithe.

"Will a mere mortal rob God? Yet you rob me.

"But you ask, 'How are we robbing you?'

"In tithes and offerings. You are under a curse—your whole nation—because you are robbing me. Bring the whole tithe into the store-house, that there may be food in my house. Test me in this," says the LORD Almighty, "and see if I will not throw open the floodgates of heaven and pour out so much blessing that there will not be room enough to store it."

So God cursed them because they were not tithing, right?

No, that is not what the passage says. The Israelites were the ones who broke the covenant. By doing so, they put themselves out on their own and became open game for the enemy. The curse was purely the automatic consequence of disobedience and breaking covenant with God.

Malachi 3:10 says, "'Test me in this,' says the LORD Almighty, 'and see if I will not throw open the floodgates of heaven and pour out so much blessing that there will not be room enough to store it.'" That is a straight-up challenge from God. Try Me. Prove Me. Test Me.

"Well, I tried Him for two weeks, but nothing happened."

Oh, come on. Walk faithfully in it. Come back and see me in a year. Try to tell me things are worse off than before. Try to tell me God is a liar. Anyone is welcome to take me up on that challenge because I know what is going to happen.

God wants to open the floodgates on your life. Have you ever seen Hoover Dam or another truly enormous dam? When they open the flood-gates on dams like that, throngs of people show up with cameras. The vast quantity of water suddenly rushing through makes for an amazing sight. That is the picture God gives us in Malachi. He is just dying to pull the lever and let vast quantities of His blessings rush through into your life.

The sad truth is most Christians do not believe that. Some surveys have estimated as much as 87 percent of Christians who regularly attend church do not tithe. They keep God from doing what He wants to do—pour out His blessing on their lives.

The very end of that passage in Malachi says, "'I will prevent pests from devouring your crops, and the vines in your fields will not drop their fruit before it is ripe,' says the LORD Almighty. 'Then all the nations will call you blessed, for yours will be a delightful land,' says the LORD Almighty" (3:11–12).

Repentance leads to victory. After the Israelites dealt with Achan and his sin, they went back to Ai. This time they wiped Ai off the map. Do you want your full inheritance? Do you want to possess absolutely everything that's yours? Bring the full tithe, and God will pour out his blessing on your life.

# Shechem

After defeating Ai, the Israelites traveled on until they reached a place called Shechem. Shechem was a narrow valley in between two mountains—Mount Ebal to the north and Mount Gerizim to the south.

Shechem was a famous and special place for Old Testament Israel. God interacted with His people in a lot of interesting and powerful ways in this tight, little valley. It was here that God renewed His covenant with Abraham. Jacob's Well, a well-known holy site for Jews and Christians alike, is also located near Shechem.

The two mountains pressed tightly against each other created a natural amphitheater. Voices carried very loudly over the whole area without any help. The entire nation of Israel gathered at Shechem many times because it was one of the best places to speak to a massive group of people before the advent of microphones and sound equipment. One of the first times they gathered there was during their campaign to take the Promised Land.

> Then Joshua built on Mount Ebal an altar to the LORD, the God of Israel, as Moses the servant of the LORD had commanded the Israelites. He built it according to what is written in the Book of the Law of Moses—an altar of uncut stones, on which no iron tool had been used. On it they offered to the LORD burnt offerings and sacrificed fellowship offerings. There, in the presence of the

Israelites, Joshua wrote on stones a copy of the law of Moses. All
the Israelites, with their elders, officials and judges, were standing
on both sides of the ark of the covenant of the LORD, facing the
Levitical priests who carried it. Both the foreigners living among
them and the native-born were there. Half of the people stood in
front of Mount Gerizim and half of them in front of Mount Ebal,
as Moses the servant of the LORD had formerly commanded when
he gave instructions to bless the people of Israel.

Afterward, Joshua read all the words of the law—the blessings and
the curses—just as it is written in the Book of the Law. There was
not a word of all that Moses had commanded that Joshua did not
read to the whole assembly of Israel, including the women and children, and the foreigners who lived among them. (Josh. 8:30–35)

Verse 31 says, "As Moses the servant of the LORD had commanded the
Israelites." Joshua was not doing something he thought up himself. He was
following very specific, detailed instructions given to him by Moses. Moses
did not think these things up on his own either. God spoke to Moses and
told him what He wanted Israel to do at Shechem, and Moses passed the
commandments on to Joshua in Deuteronomy 27:1–8.

Moses ...commanded the people, "Keep all these commands that
I give you today. When you have crossed the Jordan into the land
the LORD your God is giving you, set up some large stones and coat
them with plaster. Write on them all the words of this law.... Set
up these stones on Mount Ebal.... Build there an altar to the LORD
your God, an altar of stones.... Sacrifice fellowship offerings there,
eating them and rejoicing in the presence of the LORD your God.

And you shall write very clearly all the words of this law on these stones you have set up."

So Moses instructed Joshua and the people of Israel to go to Shechem. There they were to gather some stones, coat them in plaster, write God's laws upon them, and pile them up on Mount Ebal. Take a stone, whitewash it, write the Law on it, and put it on the pile. Take another stone, coat it with plaster, write the Law on it, and put it on the pile.

Joshua 8 shows the people following Moses's directions under the leadership of Joshua. They stacked whitewashed stones on Mount Ebal, each one covered in God's laws—laws God knew Israel would never keep. They had not kept them up to that point, and they were not going to keep them, but they stacked the stones anyway. Then, according to Moses's instructions, Joshua built an altar right in the middle of those stones.

This is a picture of the cross. Before Christ came into our lives, you and I were nothing more than whitewashed stones at best. We were all white and pretty on the outside. We put on a good face, doing this and doing that. But on the inside? Not so pretty. Not so white and clean. We were whitewashed. The Law was written on the outside of us, but it had not yet been written on our hearts. We were like the Pharisees. Jesus called them "whitewashed tombs" to their faces (Matt. 23:27). In other words, you are all pretty and white on the outside, but inside you are nothing but rotting bones.

Whitewashing is the essence of religion. That is what religion always does. That is what religion is.

"Wait a minute. I thought Christianity was a religion."

No, it isn't. Real, biblical Christianity is the complete opposite of religion. Religion is following a list of dos and don'ts. Religion is cleaning the outside and expecting the inside to change sooner or later. Let me give you a hint: the inside has never changed because of anything done to the outside. It never has, and it never will. Religion tries to work from the outside in. Christianity works from the inside out. God changes our hearts, and slowly—sometimes very slowly—those changes work their way to the outside.

God knew the Israelites were not going to live up to the Law. At Shechem, He had them build an altar smack-dab in the middle of a bunch of whitewashed stones covered in the Law. That altar was a picture of the cross. Today, the cross stands right in the middle of our failure to live the way God called us to live.

The apostle Paul referred to Shechem and the Law when he said, "And you, being dead in your trespasses and the uncircumcision of your flesh, He has made alive together with Him, having forgiven you all trespasses, having wiped out the *handwriting of requirements* that was against us, which was contrary to us. And He has taken it out of the way, having nailed it to the cross" (Colossians 2:13–14 NKJV, italics added).

Under the Law, we had to be perfect and have everything perfect. Have you lived a perfect life? Have you responded perfectly to every situation? Even when you have done good things, have you done them all out of perfect motivations?

Shechem is a picture of what Jesus did for you and me. He dealt with our failure to live out the Law. We failed to live life perfectly, but Jesus took that failure away from us at the cross. He removed it from our lives along with the curse that came from not living perfectly.

God instructed Joshua to put the altar right in the middle of the pile of whitewashed stones, which represented the Law. God was saying, "I am right in the middle of this thing, and I am big enough to fix it. I am big enough to wipe it all out."

God is in the middle of all your failures, and He is big enough to fix every one of them. Everything you did that you should not have done? God is big enough to fix it. Everything you did not do that you should have done? He will wipe it all out and give you a totally clean slate.

Let me give you another story from my prison ministry. One time the prison gave us forty guys and allowed us to do four full days of ministry. We saw God do some incredible things in that time. Roughly half of those forty men experienced dramatic, wonderful change in their lives.

During the third day, one of the guys we were ministering to came up to me. I had been watching him a lot. He had mostly just been listening and observing. I think for the first couple of days he was just looking for our angle. He did not trust us because he did not understand why we were there. When he finally figured out we were just there to help, he started to open up. God began to touch his heart. I saw his eyes well up with tears several times during the second and third days.

On the third day, this man walked straight up to me during one of the breaks. He was a really big guy. He could have snapped me like a toothpick if he wanted to, and that was more than a little intimidating. But he walked up to me, tears in his eyes, and said, "Myles, I understand what you're saying. I see it clearly, but there is no way God could forgive me."

"That's impossible. You're not hearing what we're telling you. God will forgive you no matter what you've done," I said.

"You don't know what I've done," he said. "Let me tell you—"

"No, don't tell me," I said. "I don't need to know. It doesn't matter what you've done. It doesn't matter where you've been. None of that matters. There is nothing too big for God. There is nothing He can't erase."

"There is no way God can take this out of my life."

I realized later this was probably not the smartest thing to do, but at that moment, I looked at him and said, "You are the most prideful, arrogant person I have ever met in my life."

He took about a half step back. "What'd you say to me?"

"You heard me. You are the most prideful, arrogant person I have ever met in my life."

"Why are you saying that?" he said. At this point, he was irritated, a little mad.

"Because it's true. I have never met anybody as prideful and arrogant as you. You think that somehow or another you can scratch something in the stone that God Himself cannot erase. How big a boy do you think you are? You think you can put a stain in your garment that the blood of Jesus can't wash out."

Right in the midst of your failure, God put a cross. Right in the middle of every mess you have ever made, God put a cross. The blood of Jesus is there. Blessings and life are there in that very place.

"Myles, you don't know what I've done! You don't know how many times I've screwed up! There is a mountain of things that I have failed in and messed up."

It doesn't matter how high your mountain of curses and failures is; the cross stands right in the middle of all of it.

If you read the rest of Deuteronomy 27, you will find that Moses gave more instructions to Joshua and the people of Israel regarding Shechem. After he described the whitewashed stones and the altar, Moses told Joshua to select twelve representatives, one from each of the twelve tribes of Israel. Six of those representatives were to stand on Mount Ebal, and the other six were to stand on Mount Gerizim. The rest of the people, a multitude of tens of thousands, were to stand in the valley between the two mountains. The representatives standing on Mount Ebal were to shout down curses on the people while the representatives standing on Mount Gerizim were to shout down blessings.

The Bible does not tell us exactly how this was done. Did all the representatives yell simultaneously? Did the ones on Mount Ebal shout a curse, then wait for the ones on Mount Gerizim to shout a blessing that counter-acted the curse? I think it is probably the latter, but no one knows for sure.

Either way, it would have been a surreal situation. It reminds me of what fans sometimes do at sports games. I am a University of Texas fan, so I think of UT games. Aggies, you will just have to forgive me for this illustration. At UT games, the crowd on one side of the court or stadium shouts, "TEXAS!" Then all the people on the other side shout, "FIGHT!" Back and forth, over and over. "TEXAS!" "FIGHT!"

I think that must have been what this situation was like, just on a much grander scale. Tens of thousands of people standing together. One side, "CURSES!" Then the other side, "BLESSINGS!"

Can you imagine what was going through their heads? I think I can. *What on earth is going on here? What is God trying to say to us, if anything?*

Things become clear when we look at the rest of Deuteronomy. The instructions for what to do at Shechem came from Deuteronomy 27. Moses goes on to list the blessings and curses of God in Deuteronomy 28–29. Through Moses, God was saying, "If you walk in my ways, here are the blessings that will flow into your life. If you do not walk in my ways, here are the curses that will naturally come on your life." Then those chapters flow right into Deuteronomy 30, which can be summed up in one word: *choose*. Deuteronomy 30:19 says, "This day I call the heavens and the earth as witnesses against you that I have set before you life and death, blessings and curses. Now choose."

Choose blessings, or choose curses. Choose life, or choose death.

What was the meaning of Shechem? Shechem was the valley of deci-sion. Shechem was the place of choosing. Life or death. Blessings or curses. Choose abundant life, or choose to just live life. Take your pick.

To this very day, Mount Ebal—where the curses came from—is a barren mountain. On the other side, Mount Gerizim—where the blessings came from—is green and lush.

The last chapter of Joshua mirrors the truth of Shechem. When Joshua was about to die, he could see that the people of God were already beginning to stray and walk away from God and His ways. He sent word throughout Israel and gathered all the people together in one place again. Then he spoke to them, saying, "Choose for yourselves this day whom you will serve. But as for me and my household, we will serve the Lord" (Josh. 24:15). Can you guess where Joshua gathered the people together? At Shechem. He called all of Israel back to the same place to tell them the same thing.

Choose life, or choose death. Choose blessings, or choose curses. Me? My family? We are going to be wise. We are going to choose life. We are going to choose blessings.

Here is the truth we must learn from Shechem: you can choose. The same choices are before us today. You can choose life, or you can choose death. You can choose blessings, or you can choose curses. You get to choose. You can choose for yourself, you can choose for your marriage, you can choose for your family, and you can choose for your ministry. You make the choice.

To clarify what I mean by *ministry*, I am not just talking about what you do at church. We have narrowed the meaning of that word, but ministry is so much more than what happens within the four walls of the local church. Ministry is what happens in your workplace. Ministry is what happens in your home. Anything God has called you to do is ministry in your life. You can choose to walk out that ministry in a way that brings life and blessings, or you can choose to walk out that ministry in a way that brings death and curses.

Galatians 5:1 says, "It is for freedom that Christ has set us free." Jesus set you free so that you would have the freedom to choose. Not freedom to do whatever you want to do, but freedom to do what you ought to do. Because of Christ, you now can choose life. Because of Christ, you now have the ability to choose blessing. It is your decision.

If you are going to possess all that God has for you, it is not enough to simply get saved. It is not enough to simply be filled with the Spirit. If you are going to walk in the promises God has given you, you have to make good decisions.

Don't be arrogant and say, "I'm born again. I'm filled with the Spirit. But I am not going to do what God told me to do." If you do, you are not going to get what God wants you to have. You have got to make good decisions in life. There are consequences to all of the choices we make.

My apologies to Doris Day, but she was completely wrong. "Que Sera, Sera (Whatever Will Be, Will Be)."[15] Bull corn! Great song, but Doris missed it. We get different results in life depending on the decisions we make. We can make these decisions and go this way, or we can make those decisions and go that way.

Through the cross, God provided a way of blessing. But to experience that blessing we must choose to walk in His path of blessing. The path will always be there, but every day we choose whether or not we walk in it.

Do you want the blessings of God in your life? Of course you do. Who doesn't? The real question is, are you willing to walk in the path God prescribed every day? Are you willing to walk daily in the path of blessing God has provided for you?

So many born-again believers are not walking in God's path of blessing. They do not receive the blessings of God because they do not walk the way He instructed us to walk.

The Bible is a love letter to you and me. It shows us how to walk in God's ways. God did not leave us to sit in the dark and wonder, "How do I do life? How do I do marriage? How do I do work? How do I relate to other people in a life-giving way?" The Bible is a blessing because it gives us the ability to learn how to walk in God's pathway of blessing in every area of our lives.

If you decide not to walk in the pathway prescribed by the Bible, don't shake your fist at God and say, "I thought You loved me." He does love you, but you chose to walk a different path.

"So I just have to walk in God's pathway of blessing? That's it? Then everything will be wonderful and I will never have any problems anymore?"

No, that is not what I'm saying! We live in a fallen world. Bad things happen to good people in a fallen world. The Bible says it rains on the just and the unjust (Matt. 5:45). You will experience trouble and problems whether you are righteous or not. But if you are walking in God's pathway of blessing, you will always have abundant life. Even when bad things bring sorrow and hardship, you will still experience peace and joy.

God never said He would deliver us out of every problem. He just promised to meet us in the problems and walk through them with us. Those are two very different things.

When people come to me for counseling or advice, most of the time it is because they have a big problem or awful situation in their lives. They tell me all about the problem or the situation, then I usually ask some questions and try to clarify what is happening. When we get to the end of all that, they almost always have a certain expectation. Some people speak it. Others just think it. Either way, the expectation is this: "You have my problem. Now fix it. You know about my situation. Now solve it." Do you know how I respond?

"If we could just get the right person to pray for you, with the right music and lights at the perfect level—oh man. Everything would get better."

That is charismatic nuttiness. That is not from the Bible, and it is not what I say.

Here is what I say to every single person who comes to me with a problem: "I don't fix problems. I don't solve situations. I have no magic wand in my back pocket. But let me tell you what I can do. I can give you a path to walk, a path that comes straight from the Bible. If you walk that path and stay on it, then you will wind up in a very different place from where you are today. You are going to love that place because it is wonderful. Just stay on the path."

Let me be very clear with you right now. You cannot walk your own path and end up in God's blessings. People have tried that over and over. That has never worked, and it never will. Proverbs 27:12 says, "The wise see trouble ahead and avoid it, but the foolish keep going and suffer for it." There are two kinds of people here—the wise and the foolish. Both the wise and the foolish see the trouble, but they respond in completely different ways.

Wise people see the trouble ahead and make a course correction. They see what is coming and say, "You know what? I don't want to end up there. That's not what I want for my life. I don't care what it takes, I'm going to find a different path so I end up at a different destination."

Wise people understand Shechem. Wise people understand the valley of decision.

Foolish people look right at the trouble coming and think, "Oh, that looks like pain. That looks like a mess. Golly, I really don't want that." Then they keep walking toward it, run straight into it, and blame God when things go wrong.

Why do they do that? In my experience, most often people keep walking down the path toward trouble because they struggle with one of three different issues. Sometimes they just don't want to face reality. They want to plow on through life, *que sera, sera.*

Sometimes they have not yet come to a place of maturity. Young people, please listen closely to this one. Older people, please don't skip this part. There is no age limit on maturity. Immature people are those who do not connect the dots in life. There is a connection between what you do today and what you get tomorrow. Immature people do not make that connection. They do not realize the decisions they make today affect where they go in life.

Babies do not think past what is happening right now. Only once they become young children, five or six years old, they start thinking past the moment to maybe the next hour or two. That is the beginning of maturity. Then, as they get older, more maturity comes, and they start to connect the dots of life further and further out. They start thinking about how their decisions today will affect the rest of the month. Then they connect the dots for maybe the rest of the year. Then, if they keep growing in maturity as they reach adulthood, they start thinking about how their decisions and actions will affect their lives fifteen, twenty, thirty, even forty years down the road. That is maturity. Without maturity, people tend to keep walking down whatever path they are already on because they do not connect the dots.

Other times people keep walking down the path toward trouble because they believe something. They see what is coming down the road, but they keep going because they believe that they are the first exception to the rule in human history. I am going to be the first one to walk this path and end up at a different and better destination. Watch and see!

That is foolishness.

Listen to me, beloved of God. If you are on a path toward trouble in any area of your life, make a course correction. Even if most of your life is good, if you see trouble coming anywhere, now is the time to change the way you are walking. Make good decisions.

Many times people have asked me how Sallie and I ended up with such an incredible marriage. How did it happen? We did not just wake up one day with a good marriage. We made good decisions. Every time there was a marriage conference, we went to it. Even if we already had plans or we were just tired, we went to it. I cannot tell you how many good books on marriage we have read together. That is the path we walked, and we ended up in a good place.

If you are off course in any area of your life—your marriage, your work, your relationships, or anywhere else—change your direction. Then give it some time because there is always a delay in the process. To say, "I made a decision to change on Sunday, but now it's Wednesday, and I don't see any change. You know what? Forget it!" is bean-sprout faith. Do you know what bean-sprout faith is? Think about kids in elementary school. When teachers teach kids about how plants grow, what do they typically use? Bean seeds. Each kid takes a little cup, puts some soil in it, plants a bean seed, and waters it. Within a matter of days, the seed sprouts and the seedling pokes through the soil. Kids would have trouble waiting much longer than the few days.

That is the extent of many people's faith. If they do not see growth in a matter of days after they plant, they throw the whole thing out. Here is the problem: most of the time growth takes a lot longer than that.

Chart a different course. If you are not experiencing God's blessings and abundance in an area of your life, then stop, back up, evaluate that area, and ask questions. How did I end up here? What decisions and actions put me in this place? It is time to shift gears and make some different decisions. Get on God's path, then stay on that path and do not let anything knock you off. If you get knocked down, just get back up and stay on the path.

God wants you to walk in His pathway of blessing. He is a good Father who gave you His Word to provide that path for you. Psalm 119:105 says, "Your word is a lamp for my feet, a light on my path." What path? The pathway of blessing, the pathway of life.

If you are serious about possessing what's yours, then you have to understand Shechem. You have to choose blessing. You have to choose life. You have to make good decisions. Then you have to keep going. Eugene Peterson—quoting Friedrich Nietzsche—called it "a long obedience in the same direction."[16] Stay on the path.

As for me and my house, we choose every day to walk in God's ways— His pathway of blessing for our lives. Each day we choose life instead of death. Every day we choose blessings instead of curses. Each day we choose abundant life rather than just life.

# Gibeon

Possessing your inheritance is going to be a battle.

You have a destiny and a purpose in God. He wants you to live a life full of His blessings and promises. Do you want to possess those things? You're going to have to take them. It's going to be a fight. If you are to possess your full inheritance, then you have to believe your inheritance is worth fighting for.

After Israel passed through Shechem, they faced the rest of the Promised Land. Joshua 9 tells us what happened next.

Now when all the kings west of the Jordan heard about these things—the kings in the hill country, in the western foothills, and along the entire coast of the Mediterranean Sea as far as Lebanon (the kings of the Hittites, Amorites, Canaanites, Perizzites, Hivites and Jebusites)— they came together to wage war against Joshua and Israel.

However, when the people of Gibeon heard what Joshua had done to Jericho and Ai, they resorted to a ruse: They went as a delegation whose donkeys were loaded with worn-out sacks and old wineskins, cracked and mended. They put worn and patched sandals on their feet and wore old clothes. All the bread of their food supply was dry and moldy. Then they went to Joshua in the camp at Gilgal and said to him and the Israelites, "We have come from a distant country; make a treaty with us."

The Israelites said to the Hivites, "But perhaps you live near us, so how can we make a treaty with you?"

"We are your servants," they said to Joshua.

But Joshua asked, "Who are you and where do you come from?"

They answered: "Your servants have come from a very distant country because of the fame of the LORD your God. For we have heard reports of him: all that he did in Egypt, and all that he did to the two kings of the Amorites east of the Jordan—Sihon king of Heshbon, and Og king of Bashan, who reigned in Ashtaroth. And our elders and all those living in our country said to us, 'Take provisions for your journey; go and meet them and say to them, "We are your servants; make a treaty with us."' This bread of ours was warm when we packed it at home on the day we left to come to you. But now see how dry and moldy it is. And these wineskins that we filled were new, but see how cracked they are. And our clothes and sandals are worn out by the very long journey."

The Israelites sampled their provisions but did not inquire of the LORD. Then Joshua made a treaty of peace with them to let them live, and the leaders of the assembly ratified it by oath.

Three days after they made the treaty with the Gibeonites, the Israelites heard that they were neighbors, living near them. So the Israelites set out and on the third day came to their cities: Gibeon, Kephirah, Beeroth and Kiriath Jearim. But the Israelites did not attack them, because the leaders of the assembly had sworn an oath to them by the LORD, the God of Israel.

The whole assembly grumbled against the leaders, but all the leaders answered, "We have given them our oath by the LORD, the God of Israel, and we cannot touch them now. This is what we will do to them: We will let them live, so that God's wrath will not fall on us for breaking the oath we swore to them." (Josh. 9:1–20)

This much is clear: God takes covenant seriously, even covenants made in error and deception. Israel could not break the covenant they made, but they dealt with the Gibeonites differently.

They continued, "Let them live, but let them be woodcutters and water carriers in the service of the whole assembly." So the leaders' promise to them was kept.

Then Joshua summoned the Gibeonites and said, "Why did you deceive us by saying, 'We live a long way from you,' while actually you live near us? You are now under a curse: You will never be released from service as woodcutters and water carriers for the house of my God."

They answered Joshua, "Your servants were clearly told how the LORD your God had commanded his servant Moses to give you the whole land and to wipe out all its inhabitants from before you. So we feared for our lives because of you, and that is why we did this. We are now in your hands. Do to us whatever seems good and right to you."

So Joshua saved them from the Israelites, and they did not kill them. That day he made the Gibeonites woodcutters and water carriers for the assembly, to provide for the needs of the altar of the LORD at the place the LORD would choose. And that is what they are to this day. (Josh. 9:21–27)

Joshua 9 demonstrates one thing clearly. When the people of God move forward, the enemy will always rise up.

I hope you are beginning to understand and believe that you have a calling and an inheritance in God. But know that as you move toward what God has for you, the enemy will rise up. Whenever you take a step toward possessing what is yours, expect the devil to attack.

We are playing a zero-sum game. There is no win-win situation between us and the devil. Any gain for us is a loss for him, always. When we take ground for our own, the devil loses it. Every gain we make on our inheritance comes at the enemy's expense. He is not going to roll over, play dead, and just let us take what's ours. He is going to fight us tooth and nail to keep us from possessing anything God has for us.

Israel's enemies came at them in the same way our enemy comes at us today. There are two primary ways the devil attacks us.

Sometimes the enemy goes for a face-to-face confrontational battle with us. This is the style of attack found in the first part of Joshua 9, when several of the kings of Canaan got together and formed an alliance to destroy Israel. There are times when the devil loads up all his weapons and comes at us just like that.

Most of the time, however, he attacks us in a different way. The Bible says Satan comes like a roaring lion (1 Pet. 5:8), but he also comes as a crafty serpent (Gen. 3:1). More often than not, he will come with deceit and craftiness, as the Gibeonites came to the Israelites. He wants to trick us and bring compromise into our lives that will keep us from fully possessing what God has for us.

After Israel had several victories under their belt, word got out. The Gibeonites, who lived nearby, realized, "Hey, we're next on the list. We've got to do something about this." They tricked Israel into believing they had come from a faraway country and convinced Israel to make a treaty with them, saying, "Come on, we're no harm to you. We don't even live in the land you are supposed to possess." In their craftiness, Gibeon deceived Israel and kept them from possessing all of what God said was theirs.

Why was this a problem? Because God had already commanded them not to make any covenants or treaties with the nations living in Canaan. God wanted all of the Promised Land for Israel. There was no reason to let any other people stay there. The nations of Canaan worshipped idols and sacrificed children to false gods. God knew if Israel lived in the midst of that, they would take on some of the idolatry. Down the road, that is exactly what happened because of the covenant they made with the Gibeonites.

If you are serious about possessing what is yours, then you must understand how the devil will attack you. More important, you must learn how to prevent him from deceiving you out of your inheritance. The Gibeonites represent for us how the devil comes in craftiness to steal that which is ours. He wants to trick you into compromises that rob you of your full inheritance.

Joshua 9:4 says the Gibeonites "resorted to a ruse." The New King James Version says they "worked craftily." The word there is the Hebrew word *ormah*, which comes from the word *arom*. The word *arom* literally means "to be slick or smooth," but it is most often used to figuratively describe craftiness and deceit.

We have similar terms in English. Ever heard a person call someone a smooth operator? That is not a compliment. It means you had better hold on to your wallet. Sometimes we call manipulative language "smooth talk." These ideas are in the same vein of *arom*—the craftiness of the Gibeonites and the devil.

Whenever the Word of God first mentions a significant person or concept, that first mention has more significance than any other time. Theologians call this the law of first mention. The names of God provide great examples of this law. Every time God first revealed a different name and aspect of His character to His people, He painted a beautiful picture around the revelation to give them an understanding of the depth of His character. In Exodus 15:26, the Lord revealed Himself to Israel as Jehovah-Rapha, "For I am the LORD, who heals you." This came immediately after he miraculously purified the bitter waters of Marah, giving a picture and a revelation of His power to heal.

The law of first mention is also true for other things in the Bible—people, teachings, words, and even the devil himself. Scripture mentions Satan for the first time in Genesis 3:1, "Now the serpent was more crafty than any of the wild animals." That picture is meant to show us who the devil is and how he works. The devil is a smooth operator. He is a slick dealer, a fast-talking dude.

Satan understands very well that he cannot stop God in his own power. There is absolutely no contest between his power and God's power. Some Christians believe there is a major power struggle between God and the

GIBEON

. . . .

devil, but that's not the truth. Satan's power pales in comparison to God's. Think about when you turn on the light in a dark room. The darkness does not fight the light. It does not resist all the way down the wall and say, "No! This corner's mine. I'm not going to let the light have it." The light turns on, and the darkness immediately goes. That is a representation of God's power in comparison with the devil's. When God's light comes, darkness immediately flees.

Revelation 20 describes Satan taken by the scruff of the neck, bound, and tossed into the abyss. Who does those things to him? Not Jesus. Not even Gabriel or Michael or one of the other special, powerful archangels of God. The devil is bound and tossed into the abyss by some no-name angel. God basically says, "Hey, you, Private So-and-So, go get him and toss him in there."

There is no power struggle between God and the devil. He cannot overcome God. He cannot overcome God's purposes. He cannot overcome the people of God when they are walking in obedience and righteousness. He cannot stand against the power of the blood shed on the cross or the power of the Holy Spirit. The devil cannot overpower us, and he knows that. He knows that better than we do, unfortunately. He cannot win through force, but he is far more dangerous to us in his craftiness than he is in his power.

Second Corinthians 2:10–11 says, "Anyone you forgive, I also forgive. And what I have forgiven—if there was anything to forgive—I have forgiven in the sight of Christ for your sake, so that Satan might not outwit us. For we are not unaware of his schemes." The New King James Version says it this way: "Lest Satan should take advantage of us; for we are not ignorant of his devices."

What is this verse saying? When we are aware of the way the devil works—his plans, his schemes, and his craftiness—he is not able to gain an advantage over us. The reverse is true as well. When we are ignorant of the way the devil works, he will take advantage of us.

The word translated as "advantage" is the Greek word *pleonekteó*. That word means "to hold the greater portion." If you are ignorant of the way the devil works, he will gain greater portion of your inheritance. If you are unaware of his schemes, he will gain the greater portion of your marriage and your family. If you forget how he operates, he will gain the greater portion of your life.

This principle is true corporately as well. If we, the Grace church network, do not want the devil to gain the greater portion of Southeast Texas, we need to be aware of the way he works. We need to be aware of the way he causes offenses and plays people against one another in churches. If we are ignorant of how the devil is going to move against us corporately, he will gain the greater portion of our collective inheritance.

Ephesians 6:11 says, "Put on the full armor of God, so that you can take your stand against the devil's schemes." God calls us to stand against the devil's schemes. He wants us to come against them, overthrow them, and crush them.

The word translated as "schemes" is the Greek word *methodeia*. Do you see the English word in there? The devil works in methods. The word *methodeia* literally means "the following of an orderly and systematic procedure." When the devil attempts to rob you of your inheritance, he does so in a very orderly and systematic way.

The devil does not just haphazardly fling his fiery darts out there. He does not toss a bunch of them out and hope one lands on you. He is a sharpshooter. He is looking for your Achilles' heel, and he is systematic in his approach. He does not just say, "You know, it's been a while since I've been after Carl. I forgot all about him. Let me just throw some arrows his way and see if one happens to hit."

The devil works constantly, day after day. He plots, he schemes, and he plans. He arranges circumstances, situations, and meetings. Just as God sets up divine appointments to bless us, the enemy sets up appointments for his own purposes. It can be astonishing how well he arranges things.

I once counseled a husband who was certain his wife was running around on him. He had a wonderful, godly wife who had not been unfaithful to him in any way, shape, or form. But the enemy wedged a thought of suspicion into the husband's mind, and his mind ran with it. In the space of a single week, the man became utterly convinced his wife was cheating on him.

This husband irrationally suspected four specific men. Even though he did not normally see any of them, in that one week he happened to run into every single one of those guys. One of the four was a former employee the husband had not seen in years. That former employee's car happened to break down on the husband's way to work that week. Coincidence? Sounds more like a plan of the enemy to me.

The devil schemes. He does not work off the cuff, and we need to understand that. He attacks and deceives systematically and purposefully.

Second Corinthians 11:3 says, "But I am afraid that just as Eve was deceived by the serpent's cunning, your minds may somehow be led astray from your sincere and pure devotion to Christ." The word translated as "cunning" is the Greek word *panourgia*. That word comes from two different Greek words, *pan* (all) and *ourgia* (work). *Panourgia* literally means "all work" or "all working."

In other words, the devil attacks us with all guns blazing. He comes at us fully armed with all kinds of schemes. He throws everything at us. To use a baseball analogy, the devil is like a pitcher who knows every pitch in the book, and we are called to bat against him.

When I started playing baseball at the University of Texas, I learned one thing very quickly: the pitchers were at a completely different level.

Playing for Wharton High School, every pitcher I ever went up against had only one pitch—a medium-speed fastball. At the college level, suddenly I was going up against pitchers who were not only throwing in the mid-nineties but also throwing all kinds of pitches. They had wicked sliders, curveballs that started at your head and dropped on the outside corner of the plate, fastballs that ran right in on your hands, and everything else. It was a far cry from anything I had known up to that point, and it had me wondering if I could even hang at the college level.

If you want to play at a higher level, you have to be able to hit every kind of pitch. If you want to go up to the big leagues with God, take all of your inheritance, and become all of who He destined you to be, you have to be able to hit every type of pitch the devil throws. Why? Because if you cannot hit a certain type of pitch, you are going to see it every time you come to bat.

Those college-level pitchers figured out quickly I could not hit a curveball to save my life. Can you guess what happened after that? Every time I stepped up to the plate, I got five straight curveballs. I watched a couple, whiffed the others, and sat back down. On my own time, I spent hours in the batting cage with the pitching machine set to throw me nothing but curveballs. I had to learn how to hit that pitch. Until I did, I was not going to see anything else.

The devil will throw everything he can at you. He has all kinds of ways to work your case, all kinds of crafty schemes and plans. Once he finds an area where you are weak, he will pitch to it over and over. Until you learn how to overcome, you are going to keep seeing the same thing again and again.

If you are the kind of person who is easily offended, guess what he is going to throw at you? Offense after offense after offense. Every time you get back into the saddle, a new offense will knock you down. That pitch is going to keep coming. Either you will learn to hit it, or it will prevent you from moving forward into what God has for you.

"Well, I just can't trust anybody in authority."

Then he will give you reason after reason to distrust those in authority. Until you get through that, you are not going to move on to the next level.

There are four ways we can prevent the devil's schemes from working in our lives.

## 1. THE WORD OF GOD

If we are going to stand against the schemes of the enemy, we need to have a good understanding of the Word of God. We need to read the Word, meditate on it, dig into it, and find out what God has to say.

The Bible will keep us from missing the mark. It will always line us up, straight and true. If something comes into our lives and we get off track, then we just have to come back to the Word of God and line up with it.

The Word of God helps us make decisions. I understand that there are a lot of issues in life the Word of God does not speak to specifically. The Word of God is not going to tell you whether or not you should marry Joe or take the job at General Electric. Answers like that are not in there, but there are governing principles in the Word of God that apply to every situation and decision we face.

The Word of God keeps us from being deceived. Without the Word in our lives, we will be easy pickings, ripe for the schemes of the enemy.

## 2. PRAYER

If we are going to stand against the schemes of the enemy, then our prayer lives must be strong.

Many times in my life I have found myself in a mess, thinking, "Why am I in this situation? How in the world did I get here?" Most of the time I stop, back up, and realize I never really prayed about the situation in the first place. That has been true more times than I would care to confess.

Some people go to the extreme of praying about their lives. "God, how do you want me to part my hair today? How high should I part it, and should it be to the right or to the left?"

Years ago, when I was still a young Christian, I asked God which tie to wear one day. Do you know what He told me? "I don't know. Go ask Sallie."

I do not believe God cares about which shirt you put on this morning. We do not need to pray and seek God about every single mundane life detail. Some people tend toward that extreme, but I think most of us are not in any danger of that. In fact, I think most people in the body of Christ are prone to the other extreme—we haul off and do things without seeking the counsel of the Lord. We do not pray or listen to what He has to say.

That is exactly what the Israelites did in Joshua 9. When Gibeon came, trying to deceive them into making a treaty, they "did not inquire of the LORD," (v. 14). That is a key statement in the chapter. If it is not highlighted in your Bible, you might want to highlight it. Israel did not seek the counsel of the Lord, and that caused major problems.

Psalm 91:3 says God "delivers you from the snare of the trapper" (New American Standard Bible). The devil is a trapper. He is always setting out snares for us. But God will deliver you from the snare of the trapper. A lot of people read that verse and think, "Oh, hallelujah. I'm trapped, but God is going to deliver me." That is not what the verse says. Read it in context. God was saying he will keep us from ever getting into the trap to begin with.

We need to pray, seek God, and hear what He is saying to us so that we do not get trapped in the devil's deceit.

## 3. DO NOT LEAN ON YOUR OWN UNDERSTANDING

If we are going to stand against the schemes of the devil, then we must trust God over our own understanding. This is a tough one. It comes from Proverbs 3:5, "Trust in the LORD with all your heart and lean not on your own understanding; in all your ways submit to him, and he will make your paths straight." I have broken this rule a few times in my own life, and every time I paid a big price for it.

I believe God wants us to use our minds. Why else would He give them to us? We know He is interested in our minds because Romans 12:2 instructs us to "be transformed by the renewing of your mind." God wants us to think and learn with our minds, but we cannot lean on our own understanding.

Have you ever been in a situation where everything makes sense and lines up, but something just does not feel right? Maybe the Holy Spirit gave you a sort of internal check, or maybe the Lord spoke things to you. Maybe what you felt and heard went completely against all the facts and everything you could see naturally. Have you been there before?

When you get to that place, stop. Don't go anywhere. Don't do anything until you pray through. Don't take a single step forward until God gives you a clear word. Don't lean on your own understanding.

The Israelites leaned on their own understanding in their dealings with the Gibeonites. They examined all the things that had been prepared to deceive them—the worn clothing, the old wineskins, the moldy food. The Bible says they went so far as to sample the rotting provisions. They checked it all out. Everything added up ...in their own understanding.

God gave them a sense that something was not quite right. Do you remember what they said? "But perhaps you live near us, so how can we make a treaty with you?" (Josh. 9:7). Where did that question come from?

How did they know? God was speaking to them. But even though something in them was saying, "Hold up. Something is going on here," they leaned on their own understanding and moved forward. Later on, they paid the price.

Proverbs 16:3 is a wonderful piece of Scripture I think every Christian should memorize. It says this: "Roll your works upon the LORD [commit and trust them wholly to Him; He will cause your thoughts to become agreeable to His will, and] so shall your plans be established and succeed" (Amplified Bible, Classic Edition).

Commit and trust everything to God, and He will cause you to think the way He thinks. Then He will bless you, and you will have great success in all you do. Why? Because the decisions you make will be from Him. You will be thinking His thoughts, and He will lead you to do what He wants you to do.

## 4. GIRD UP THE LOINS OF YOUR MIND

If we are going to stand against the schemes of the devil, then we cannot let our minds wander loosely.

1 Peter 1:13 says, "Therefore gird up the loins of your mind" (NKJV). That appears to be a very odd phrase until you look at the context it was written in. When Peter wrote those words, almost everyone wore long, flowing robes. They could not run or move quickly without first pulling up all the loose folds of their clothing and tying them together tightly. They had to gird up their robes to run without getting entangled or tripping.

Peter was saying we should do the same thing with our minds. Do not let your mind drift lazily around. A loose mind is the devil's playground. If you spend a lot of time daydreaming and letting your thoughts run, then you are vulnerable to the enemy.

That is what the devil's fiery darts are—thoughts. He throws thoughts lit up with the fires of hell. His goal is to plant those fiery darts in your mind, and if your mind is loose, the thoughts will grow. You might spend twenty minutes or an hour or a whole day rolling one of them around in your head before you stop and ask, "Where did that even come from?"

Gird up the loins of your mind. Pay attention to what you think about. Do not have a lazy mind. Keep a short account of your thoughts. Know where each one comes from. Did that thought come from you? Was it a fiery dart from the devil? Or did it come from God?

God often speaks through the mind, especially for those young in the faith. The voice of the Lord seldom comes as a sound we can audibly hear with our ears. Usually, it comes as an intersecting thought. He simply drops a word, a picture, a memory, or something else into our minds.

You might find yourself thinking, "Where did that come from? How in the world did I end up on this topic?" God spoke to you. You were sitting there thinking about something totally different, then boom. He came in and just messed up your train of thought, didn't He?

But we have to be careful because the enemy does the same thing. He can also drop thoughts into your mind. If you let your mind flow freely all over the place, one of his fiery darts might just put you on an entirely different train of thought. That is not a train you want to be on.

Keep a short account of what is going on in your mind. When a thought comes from the devil, the Word of God tells us to take it captive (2 Cor. 10:5). Snap handcuffs on it, throw it into leg irons, and cast it out. "Get out of here! I'm not buying into that. I'm not even going to think about it. That's a bunch of nonsense."

Imagine the devil did his work by dropping into your mind and saying things like, "Hey. It's me, the devil. I think you are a no-good loser who will never amount to anything." Would any Christian listen to that? Not likely.

We know the devil is a liar. Unfortunately, he does not work that way. The devil deceives. He comes in craftiness and drops thoughts into our minds. Like, "Oh yeah, she did say that during worship practice the other day. I think she meant I'm not really flowing with the rest of the worship team. I think she meant I'm not capable of being on the worship team. Maybe I'm really not."

That thought didn't come from you. Gird up the loins of your mind. Be aware of what you are thinking and where your thoughts are coming from. Take every thought captive to the obedience of Christ.

There is one more truth I want to share with you from the story of Israel and the Gibeonites in Joshua 9. What ultimately happened to the Gibeonites? The Israelites could not destroy them because of their oath, but they did use the Gibeonites for the altar of God. Joshua told the Gibeonites, "You are now under a curse: You will never be released from service as wood-cutters and water carriers for the house of my God" (Josh. 9:23).

For this entire chapter, I have been comparing the Gibeonites to the devil and how he works in our lives. The comparison rings true here. With the Gibeonites and their deception, God foreshadowed what he was going to do with the devil. Over one thousand years later, God used the craftiness and deception of the devil to build an altar.

Without knowing it, the enemy got the world ready for God's own purposes. The devil deceived Rome, then God used Roman soldiers and leaders. The devil deceived the Pharisees, then God used the Pharisees. God let the devil work in all of his crafty ways, but He was not letting the devil win. The enemy just got the wood ready, building the altar for God's Son. The devil's deception served God's purposes.

You may have been deceived by the devil in the past. I might go so far as to say every single person has been deceived by the devil in the past. He has schemed. He has strategized. He has tricked. He has worked your case.

He has systematically attacked your life. Let this be an encouragement to you: God can take the times when you were deceived by the enemy and use them for His purposes. It is not good that you were deceived, but God can use those moments in your life to reveal things to you, train you, and prepare you for the next round. God can take those experiences and, as He sets you free, use them to build an altar in your life and bring you to the cross.

# The Power of a Covenant

Very soon after the Gibeonites deceived Israel into making a covenant with them, they called on Israel to honor it.

Now Adoni-Zedek king of Jerusalem heard that Joshua had taken Ai and totally destroyed it, doing to Ai and its king as he had done to Jericho and its king, and that the people of Gibeon had made a treaty of peace with Israel and had become their allies. He and his people were very much alarmed at this, because Gibeon was an important city, like one of the royal cities; it was larger than Ai, and all its men were good fighters. So Adoni-Zedek king of Jerusalem appealed to Hoham king of Hebron, Piram king of Jarmuth, Japhia king of Lachish and Debir king of Eglon. "Come up and help me attack Gibeon," he said, "because it has made peace with Joshua and the Israelites."

Then the five kings of the Amorites—the kings of Jerusalem, Hebron, Jarmuth, Lachish and Eglon—joined forces. They moved up with all their troops and took up positions against Gibeon and attacked it.

The Gibeonites then sent word to Joshua in the camp at Gilgal: "Do not abandon your servants. Come up to us quickly and save us!

Help us, because all the Amorite kings from the hill country have joined forces against us."

So Joshua marched up from Gilgal with his entire army, including all the best fighting men. The LORD said to Joshua, "Do not be afraid of them; I have given them into your hand. Not one of them will be able to withstand you."

After an all-night march from Gilgal, Joshua took them by surprise. The LORD threw them into confusion before Israel, so Joshua and the Israelites defeated them completely at Gibeon. Israel pursued them along the road going up to Beth Horon and cut them down all the way to Azekah and Makkedah. As they fled before Israel on the road down from Beth Horon to Azekah, the LORD hurled large hailstones down on them, and more of them died from the hail than were killed by the swords of the Israelites.

On the day the LORD gave the Amorites over to Israel, Joshua said to the LORD in the presence of Israel:

> "Sun, stand still over Gibeon,
>    and you, moon, over the Valley of Aijalon."
> So the sun stood still,
>    and the moon stopped,
>    till the nation avenged itself on its enemies,

as it is written in the Book of Jashar.

The sun stopped in the middle of the sky and delayed going down about a full day. There has never been a day like it before or since, a day when the LORD listened to a human being. Surely the LORD was fighting for Israel!

Then Joshua returned with all Israel to the camp at Gilgal. (Josh. 10:1–15)

I want to point out three things from this passage of Scripture.

## 1. GOD TOOK THE COVENANT SERIOUSLY

God took the covenant Israel made with Gibeon seriously. In fact, He took it so seriously He was not content to just sit around and watch the proceedings. When Israel moved to keep their covenant with Gibeon, God got involved.

God threw hailstones down on the Amorites. The Bible says God killed more men with His hailstones than the Israelites killed with their swords. I am guessing God has pretty good aim.

The Israelites knew God was the reason they were winning because they could see His work visibly in the natural world. God does the same thing for us today, but we often miss it because He works in the spiritual world. When we engage in prayer and spiritual warfare, we think we are putting the whoop on the enemy. Not really. God was knocking them out by the dozens while we were picking them off one by one.

God did not just throw hailstones from heaven. He also gave Joshua and the armies of Israel extra daylight. Joshua prayed and asked God to cause the sun to stand still.

Now we know Joshua had his facts a little mixed up. The sun does not move; it is the earth that turns around it. But God is not concerned when the details of our prayers are a bit wrong. When we throw our prayers up there, sometimes God reworks them before answering.

Joshua said, "God, cause the sun to stand still!"

God thought, "Well, I know what he wants. He wants more daylight. I'll just hold the earth in its place for a little bit."

Regardless, God got intimately involved in the battle. He honored the covenant between Israel and Gibeon. Remember, God had strongly commanded Israel not to make any covenants with anyone in the Promised Land. In Joshua 9, they made the covenant with Gibeon in disobedience to God. Yet here, in Joshua 10, God honored it. And it was not a grudging honor from afar. God got right in the middle of everything. God took the covenant very seriously.

Just over four hundred years after these events in Joshua, the nation of Israel went through a terrible famine for three long years. David was king at the time, and he knew something was wrong. He got on his face before God and cried out, asking to know the reason for the famine. God said, "It is on account of Saul and his blood-stained house; it is because he put the Gibeonites to death" (2 Sam. 21:1).

Saul broke the covenant Israel made with Gibeon in Joshua's day. Because of Saul's actions, God withheld rain from the whole nation for three years. Once David made things right, God gave them rain again.

For those of us who live in America, our ancestors made more than 250 treaties with the Native Americans who lived here first. Do you know how many of those treaties we, as a people, have broken? More than 250. Throughout history, we have pretty much broken every single treaty ever made with any of the people who called this land home.

Today, many white Americans have chosen to visit American Indian tribes and ask for forgiveness on behalf of our ancestors. Some people have a problem with that. "We didn't have anything to do with the breaking of those treaties. We haven't done anything against the Native Americans. Not our fault, and not our problem. Why should we apologize?"

David and his generation had nothing to do with what Saul did to the Gibeonites. They still experienced the consequences, and David had to make things right before God took the curse off of the land.

God takes all covenants seriously. That is good news for us. When Jesus poured out His life, He was serious about honoring his end of the covenant with us. When we give our lives to Jesus and walk the bloodstained path he made for us, God is serious about living up to his end of the deal. If God honored an earthly covenant made in error and deception and disobedience, how much more must he honor the covenant he made with us through the blood of his son?

## 2. JOSHUA AND THE PEOPLE OF ISRAEL TOOK THE COVENANT SERIOUSLY

The minute Joshua got word that the five kings were attacking the Gibeonites, he gathered the army. They marched all night, and then they engaged a massive Amorite army in battle. That is no small feat.

Gibeon had just deceived them into making the covenant, but Joshua and the people of Israel chose to honor it. They took the covenant seriously.

Think with me for a moment. Put yourself in Joshua's shoes.

"Sir, I have news to report."

"Yes, lieutenant?"

"Five Canaanite kings have just laid siege to Gibeon. They are going to wipe out the Gibeonites."

I would have been tempted to say, "Hmm. Getting what they deserve. Serves them right, deceiving us the way they did. You know what? This is probably God's way of getting us out of this covenant we should never have gotten into to begin with. The Gibeonites will be wiped out, and then we won't be obliged to them anymore."

That's not what Joshua said. He said, "We made a covenant, and it's time to go fight. Their enemies are our enemies."

They went and defended Gibeon. The people of Israel laid down their lives for them.

We are talking about integrity. More specifically, we are talking about integrity to covenant relationships. Psalm 15:1–4 gives us a picture of what integrity looks like.

O LORD, who may abide in Your tent?
Who may dwell on Your holy hill?
He who walks with integrity, and works righteousness,
And speaks truth in his heart.
He does not slander with his tongue,
Nor does evil to his neighbor....
He swears to his own hurt and does not change. (NASB)

He does not backbite. He does his neighbor no wrong. He makes a covenant, and when the covenant does not work out the way he thought it would—even if it costs him, even if it hurts—he does not change. That is integrity. The Living Bible says a man of integrity "keeps a promise even if it ruins him," (15:4).

Do you have a destiny in God? Yes. Has God promised things to you, through His Word and prophetically? Yes. But if you want to live in that destiny and possess those promises, you must act with integrity in the covenant relationships you are in.

"Oh, I want the promises of God! Hallelujah, they are yes and amen for me today!"

Keep dancing and shouting and praising God. You ain't gonna get anything. You will come up empty at the end of the day if you do not get this right. God gave us this story in Joshua and showed us this principle because He wants us to understand. He wants us to learn to do things His way.

Act with integrity in the covenant relationship you have with God. Act with integrity in the covenant relationship you have with your spouse. Act with integrity in the covenant relationships you have with others in the body of Christ. God has planted you in all of those relationships, and if you do not handle them with integrity, you will not get what's yours.

## 3. THE GIBEONITES TOOK THE COVENANT SERIOUSLY

Joshua 10:6 says, "The Gibeonites then sent word to Joshua in the camp at Gilgal: 'Do not abandon your servants. Come up to us quickly and save us! Help us, because all the Amorite kings from the hill country have joined forces against us.'"

The Gibeonites took the covenant seriously enough to ask for help. "Hey, we need you to drop everything and come help us! We made a covenant. Yes, we know we just deceived you. That was kind of a bad deal. But we are in need! March all night if you have to. Please, save us."

As Christians in the body of Christ today, we need to understand that the covenant blessings of the Lord are released to us when those we are in covenant with come to our aid. That is not the only way we get the covenant blessings of God, but it is one of the main ways.

"I want all of what God has for me!"

You are not going to get everything He has for you unless you come into covenant with others and allow them to meet your needs. Some of His covenant blessings are not going to come to you in any other way.

Why did God design things to work that way? Because, like many of us, God wants a nice, happy family. In my house, I like it when all of my children are happy with each other. I like it when they get along together. I also like it when they have to depend on each other to receive certain things. That keeps them working together in the flow of unity and harmony. God does the same thing for His family, the Church.

A number of years ago, I read a story about a Baptist pastor who was transferred to a little church in the middle of nowhere. He had been pastoring some good-sized churches, so he was not happy about being stuck in such a tiny place. But he obeyed and pastored the church.

About a month after he arrived, the time came for the church's annual baptism service. The new pastor spoke up about it and suggested they start baptizing people every other week, but the church members explained to him very quickly that they had some traditions they were in no mood to change.

According to the tradition, they did the baptism service at a lake on the edge of town. It was still early spring, so the weather was quite cold. They built a fire by the edge of the lake, and the church members gathered around the fire while the new believers went into the lake one by one to be baptized by the pastor.

When the new pastor finished with the last baptism, he got out of the water and joined everyone by the fire. Then he found out the next part in that church's traditional baptism service. There, around the fire, one of the members of the church introduced to the congregation all the people who had just been baptized. After each one had been introduced, the members of the congregation began introducing themselves.

"Hi, I'm so-and-so. I'm married, I have three kids, and I work at the grocery store in town. I have a car, so if you ever need a ride somewhere, I'm here for you."

"Hi, I'm so-and-so. I'm married, and I have two children. My wife and I, we don't have much, but if you ever need babysitters, we're here for you."

"Hi, I'm so-and-so. I'm married. My wife and I don't have any kids yet. If you ever need prayer or someone to talk to, we're here for you."

You get the picture. It went on and on through the whole church. Everyone had something to offer.

When I read that story, I thought, "Now this is church." That's not all of what church is, but that's a big part of it. Covenant relationships are the means by which God provides some of His covenant blessings to us.

Many years ago, doctors gave Sallie and me some sobering news about our newborn son, Daniel. After an ordeal of examinations and tests, they told us, "Take him home, but try not to get too attached. He's going to die within thirty days."

We took him home, but we refused to receive what the doctors told us. We rebuked it and chose to stand in faith. God gave us great peace, but we were still blindsided—a little dazed and a little confused.

We called several people as soon as we got home that day and asked for their prayers. They called others, and then those people called others. That afternoon my phone rang.

"You need to be at the church tonight. I know Sallie has to stay home with Daniel, but you need to come."

I was there. Many, many members of the church came that night. We worshipped in warfare on behalf of Daniel as a church body. Sometimes people came forward to intercede and pray, then we would go back into more worship. I sat there and cried through the whole thing.

After we had been there for quite a while, a young man, who had only recently been saved, came forward. That is one of the first times I ever remember his getting up in front of the congregation. He took the mic and said, "This is all wrong." That took everybody by surprise. "This is wrong. We're doing the right thing, but we're in the wrong place. We need to be in the Sweeneys' front yard."

Nods of agreement went around the room. We all loaded quietly into our cars and drove to my house. Sallie came and stood, holding Daniel, by the front window in our dining room. People trampled our flower bed and stood all around the front yard. We filled up most of that yard, even as a young church. There we prayed and worshipped and sang. When everybody left that night and my tears finally dried up—didn't think they ever would—I told Sallie, "Something's happened. Something's changed. God is going to meet us here."

That day, Sallie and I experienced the covenant blessings of God in a powerful way, and they came through our covenant relationships with others. God did meet us there. Through His miraculous power, my son lived.

Years later, we moved into a new home. So many people came to help us it looked like somebody kicked the top off a fire ant mound. Loads of stuff were coming in and going out constantly. I could only hope all of our stuff made it to the right place.

When we were unloading things at the new house, one man, a member of the church, came up to me and said, "It looks like you started painting one of those rooms."

"Yeah," I said, "but the acoustical texture on the ceiling is really thick. I've been trying to paint it with a roller, but it hasn't been working. The paint does nothing but fall on me."

"I've got a sprayer," he said. "I'll be back in a minute."

He went home, came back with his sprayer, sealed off the room, and painted the ceiling while everybody else was still unloading furniture and decorations. I thought, "Wow. This is church."

Around that time, Halloween fell on a Saturday night. The first person to arrive at the church building the next morning found a white cat with a smashed head thrown up against the front door. I called a friend of mine who happened to know some things about witchcraft and the occult. I told him we found a dead cat at the door of the church, and I asked him, "Is this for real?"

"Only if it was a white cat," he said.

"It was a white cat."

"Oh. That is either for real, or it is from somebody who knew how to copy the real thing extremely well."

From there it was not too hard to figure out what was going on. I had heard of people using witchcraft to attack churches, and I knew it was common for them to focus their efforts on the pastors, elders, and leaders. During that whole season, our entire church rallied around the pastors and elders and prayed for them.

A few months later, God gave a woman in our church a dream of somebody sacrificing a chicken. She did not understand the vision, but she shared it with me and some of the other leaders of our church. One of those leaders did some research and found out that chickens are commonly sacrificed by occultists trying to cast a death curse on someone. Again, the entire church rallied around the leaders and prayed. GCF Wharton still holds a monthly prayer service that came from this time.

In both of these times, everybody especially rallied around my family and me because I was the lead pastor and senior elder at the time. We all knew if somebody wanted to bring harm to any specific person in the church, it would most likely be me. The entire church interceded for us, breaking any power coming against us. The covenant blessings of God were released to my family and me through our covenant relationships in the body of Christ.

It is not just the big things, it is the "little" things too. I remember one time when Sallie and I were preparing to leave on a mission trip, and life was just about as hectic as it could be. We were in the middle of trip preparations, and I was trying to get way ahead in my work for my business and the church so that I would not be too far behind when we got back. Just days before we left, a church member called us and said, "I'm bringing dinner over. God put you guys on my heart, and I know you are busy right now. I have already prepared the food, and I am bringing it to your house now." Covenant blessings of God.

Sallie and I love doing marriage counseling. Counseling sessions often take up at least one or two of our nights each week. It is one thing I truly enjoy doing, especially when I get to see incredible change happening in people's lives. It absolutely thrills me.

Some of the couples we counsel have said things like this to us: "At the beginning of this, you guys committed to meeting with us one night every week for six months. We know how busy you are, and we are so grateful. Honestly, we still cannot believe you would do this for us." When they say that, I know they are just beginning to understand what it means to be in a covenant family. The covenant blessings of God are released on the couples through Sallie and me as we counsel them.

I cannot tell you how many times I have answered a late-night phone call. Sometimes it calls me to the hospital to sit and pray with someone. Sometimes it calls me to someone's house to act as a marital referee. I answer every single call I can, and in those times, I have seen God move faithfully and powerfully to meet people's needs.

I am trying to show that I have been on both sides of this deal. I have received the covenant blessings of God through others, and God has used me as a conduit to release His covenant blessings onto others.

Many of the covenant blessings of God are released to us through our covenant relationships with others. I firmly believe this truth from the Word because I have experienced it in my life. To me, this is not just a theological concept, floating out in the air somewhere. I am talking about my life, and I am talking about the life God has for all of us.

Maybe you have never experienced anything like the stories I have shared in this chapter. If you honestly cannot remember a time when you received God's covenant blessings through others, I have two questions for you.

First, have you made covenant relationships?

Please note that I am not asking you if you attend church regularly. Have you made covenant relationships? Have you planted yourself in covenant relationships with the people God has called you to be with? Have you been faithful? Have you handled those relationships with integrity? If the answer is yes, then God's blessings will flow to you.

"Well, how do you know that?"

Because that is what God says in His Word. That is His heart and His purpose, and that is one of the main things He does in and through the Church.

Second, whom did you call?

If you do not feel like you have experienced God's blessings through covenant relationships, whom did you call? The Gibeonites did not wait until somebody noticed their dire situation. They did not send up a vague flare, hoping somebody might see and come to help. They sent specific word of their specific need to Joshua and Israel.

Let me ask the question this way: To whom have you made your request clear?

Sure, it is wonderful when people meet your needs without knowing anything about them. It is great when God just drops it in someone's heart to do something that blesses you. Those are wonderful times, but they are the exceptions to the rule. The Word of God is very clear on this. If you are in need, you are responsible for speaking up and requesting help. I have a need. I need help.

If you doubt this, read your Bible. I don't care whether you like this truth or not. It is scriptural. Galatians 6:2 says, "Carry each other's burdens, and in this way, you will fulfill the law of Christ." Fulfill the law of Christ. How? By bearing one another's burdens. That does not mean just put up with one another. Sometimes we don't even do that well, but this verse asks more of us. It tells us to carry each other's burdens. Take other people's burdens on yourself and carry them away.

"But Myles, nobody is bearing my burdens for me."

Maybe nobody knows what your burdens are. Don't blame other people. Speak up and ask for help.

A lot of churchgoing people expect their brothers and sisters in Christ to be mind readers. They tell no one what they need, so those around them could meet their needs only through special words of knowledge from the Holy Spirit. That happens sometimes, but it does not happen every time.

God told us to bear one another's burdens. There is another command implied there: share your burdens with others so they can bear them for you.

James 5:14 says, "Is anyone among you sick? Let them call the elders of the church to pray over them and anoint them with oil in the name of the Lord." Are you sick? Then the elders of your church should get a word of knowledge about your illness. If they are tuned into the Spirit, they will know you are sick and visit you immediately.

That is not what the Bible says. According to the Word, the sick person should call the elders.

Are you in a covenant relationship? Do you have a need? Then make the call. If you have not called, shut up. Stop your whining and complaining. Get on the horn and let somebody know. It is incumbent upon you to make your need known clearly.

"Well, I want a new car."

I want one too. Where do we get in line for that? We all have wants and desires that may or may not be fulfilled. I am not talking about wants here. I am talking about needs.

What if somebody asks you for help? Step in and do what God tells you to do. Maybe you just need to pray for that person. Maybe you need to step forward and do something to help. Listen to God. He will never require you to do any more than what He tells you.

"I have a destiny! I have a purpose! I have blessings in God waiting for me! I have promises from God that I am going to inherit!"

True, but some of the blessings and promises God longs to give you will only come through covenant relationships. You will only receive all of what God has for you if you are willing to plug into a covenant relationship and ask for help when you need it.

There was once a father who took his young son with him to do some work outside. He told his son, "Son, you see that big boulder over there? I want you to use all of your power to move that boulder."

The son took one look at the boulder and realized he was not big enough or strong enough to move it. But his father told him to do it, so he obeyed.

The boy went over to the boulder. He pushed and struggled and strained. Before long he was sweaty and tired, but he kept pushing and shoving and trying. He began to get frustrated. Then the dad said, "Son, I want you to use all of your power."

The son said, "Dad, I'm trying! I don't understand! I can't do this!" He finally just sat down in anger and frustration. "I can't do it, Dad."

"You didn't use all of your power."

"Yes, I did! I gave it my best shot. I gave it all I had."

"No, you didn't. You didn't give it all you had. You didn't use all of your resources. You didn't use all of the power that was available to you because all you had to do was turn around and say, 'Dad, will you help me?'"

We all have boulders in our lives. Sometimes they are things God wants us to move, and sometimes they are things we want to move. Either way, the power to move our boulders is in covenant relationships. It is only through these relationships that God's complete power and blessing can flow to us.

# Makkedah

Joshua and Israel, with the direct intervention of God Himself, soundly defeated the five kings besieging Gibeon. Joshua 10:16–21 describes how their victory played out.

> Now the five kings had fled and hidden in the cave at Makkedah. When Joshua was told that the five kings had been found hiding in the cave at Makkedah, he said, "Roll large rocks up to the mouth of the cave, and post some men there to guard it. But don't stop; pursue your enemies! Attack them from the rear and don't let them reach their cities, for the LORD your God has given them into your hand."

> So Joshua and the Israelites defeated them completely, but a few survivors managed to reach their fortified cities. The whole army then returned safely to Joshua in the camp at Makkedah, and no one uttered a word against the Israelites.

The nearby nations were beginning to understand that the people of Israel were God's anointed. They knew to leave them alone. In 1 Chronicles 16:22, God says, "Do not touch my anointed ones." If you mess with God's anointed, you pay a price.

As the Church of Jesus Christ, we are God's anointed ones. We have His protection and blessing just as the Israelites did. Do we live like it? Not really. Understanding the picture in the rest of Joshua 10 might change that.

> Joshua said, "Open the mouth of the cave and bring those five kings out to me." So they brought the five kings out of the cave—the kings of Jerusalem, Hebron, Jarmuth, Lachish and Eglon. When they had brought these kings to Joshua, he summoned all the men of Israel and said to the army commanders who had come with him, "Come here and put your feet on the necks of these kings." So they came forward and placed their feet on their necks.

> Joshua said to them, "Do not be afraid; do not be discouraged. Be strong and courageous. This is what the Lord will do to all the enemies you are going to fight." Then Joshua put the kings to death and exposed their bodies on five poles, and they were left hanging on the poles until evening. (Josh. 10:22–26)

What Joshua did was common practice in ancient times, not unique to Israel. When one nation conquered another in battle, the victorious army would capture the enemy king and lay him down before their king. The victorious king would then set his foot on the enemy king's neck or head. It was a show of victory and triumph, a display of conquest. History tells us the victorious king would sometimes stand like that for hours while all of his people filed by to see.

Joshua is a type and a picture of Christ. That is not some off-the-wall claim I pulled out of midair. It is understood as fact across many different theological circles and segments of the body of Christ. In fact, Joshua's name, *Yehoshua,* is the Hebrew equivalent of the Greek name the New

Testament uses for Jesus, *Iésous*. Both words mean the same thing—Jehovah is salvation.

That brings extra meaning to this moment in Joshua 10. Joshua, as a type of Christ, displayed his conquest over the enemy. He stood with his foot on the enemy king. Thousands of years later, Jesus did the same thing. Colossians 2:15 says, "And having disarmed the powers and authorities, he [Jesus] made a public spectacle of them, triumphing over them by the cross."

Jesus triumphed over the devil at the cross. Some people are under the misconception that somehow, at some point, the devil temporarily triumphed over Jesus. That is simply not the case. The cross was not the devil getting the best of Jesus. At no point did God ever "turn the tables." Everything went His way from the beginning. Jesus got the best of the devil from the get-go. The devil did not realize what was happening until it was over and done with. He played right into God's hands.

Calvary was the mother of all championships—the Super Bowl of all eternity—and Jesus whooped the devil good. He triumphed over the enemy at the cross and made a public display of His victory. Spiritually, Jesus stood with His foot on the devil's head.

Colossians 2:15 also says Jesus "disarmed" the enemy. I like that word. It literally means to put off from, to overrun, or to overthrow. Imagine a really good football player running with the ball. I remember when Ricky Williams played for the University of Texas. When the tacklers came against him—Boom!—they got run over. The devil came like a tackler against Jesus. "I got him! I'm gonna take him down." Smack! Jesus ran right over him. He disarmed the enemy.

How about a different sports analogy? Imagine a really good pitcher in baseball. I think of Nolan Ryan. In his younger days, Ryan could pitch faster than 100 mph. He threw heat, but he was nothing compared to Jesus. If Ryan could throw 100 mph, then Jesus could spiritually throw 200 mph.

And Jesus was not playing baseball with the devil. The game was more like dodgeball. He stripped the devil of all protection—no bat, no helmet, no nothing—and beaned him with one of His supernatural fastballs.

Can you guess where the fastball hit the devil? Just look for the bruise. In Genesis 3:15, God prophetically told Satan, "And I will put enmity between you and the woman, And between your seed and her Seed; He shall bruise your head, And you shall bruise His heel" (NKJV). Jesus may have ended up with a bruised heel, but His bruise was only from crushing the devil.

Joshua was a type of Christ. He followed the customs of his day to display victory over the enemy, giving us a beautiful picture of Jesus Christ's victory over the devil.

Except Joshua did not completely follow the norm. He came close, but he did one thing very, very differently. Why? I don't think he understood why. He probably did not know exactly what he was doing, but he acted under the influence of the Holy Spirit.

Joshua said, "Bring the five kings out."

That was normal, even expected. The Israelites brought the kings out. "Lay them on the ground."

That, too, was normal. They laid the kings on the ground.

Then Joshua did something that was not at all normal. Instead of putting *his* foot on the heads of the kings, he said, "Israelites, come. Commanders, come. *You* put *your* feet on their heads."

Can you see the beautiful, vivid picture of the New Covenant here? Jesus has given you and me authority over the enemy. How much clearer can it get? How much more wonderful, powerful, and exciting? Joshua gave us the truth in bold, living color.

Jesus conquered. He won. He ran right through the enemy lines, trampled over them, and took the ball in for a touchdown. He made a public display of his victory, then He turned and said, "All right, Church. Your turn. Now you take it. You run with it. You run over the devil. You throw your fastball at him. You do it."

"Well, Jesus, that's You. I mean, You can run over people like Ricky Williams. You are the one who can throw a 200-mph fastball. I can't throw that fast."

No, no, no. You don't have to throw 200-mph fastballs. Who told you that? You need to be throwing 300-mph fastballs. Jesus said, "Very truly I tell you, whoever believes in me will do the works I have been doing, and they will do even greater things than these" (John 14:12).

"Oh, I know. I've heard that verse quoted so many times. Jesus didn't mean we are going to do the same kinds of things He did. I mean, we can't expect that. He just meant we're going to lead a lot more people to the Lord because there are so many of us now, scattered all over the world. Those are the 'greater things' He was talking about."

We do not have to guess what Jesus meant. His meaning is clear in the Greek. Interestingly enough, there are two different Greek words that both translate to the English word *greater*. One of them means greater in number, and the other means greater in quality. Can you guess which word Jesus used in that verse? We are going to do works just like His, only greater in quality.

This truth has been evident since the very beginning. We already read God's words to the serpent in Genesis 3:15, but let's go back to them in the New International Version: "And I will put enmity between you and the woman, and between your offspring and hers; he will crush your head, and you will strike his heel." When most of us read that verse, the first thing we think of is Jesus. That is not a bad thing. Jesus is the first thing we should think of. The problem is we stop there. There is much more in this verse, and we limit its meaning when we apply it only to Jesus.

In the English translations, it seems clear that God was talking about only one man. It is perfectly reasonable for us to assume that man was Jesus. But the original Hebrew is much less clear. In the phrase, "He will crush your head, and you will strike his heel," the word *he* could just as easily have been translated *they* or *she*. In fact, the King James Version says, "*It* shall bruise thy head" (italics added). In that same phrase, the word *his* is not even present in the original Hebrew. It is common to leave out a lot of pronouns in the Hebrew language, so that word was added in translation. Literally translated, the end of the verse says, "You will strike heel."

On top of that, the Hebrew word translated as *offspring* is used twice, and it is plural both times. The King James Version uses the word *seed* instead, "I will put enmity ...between thy seed [plural] and her seed [plural]." If God was only talking about Jesus, why did He use the plural form of the word?

God gave us something bigger here. He was talking about Jesus, but He was also talking about us. This might stretch you a little bit. It might go against everything you have heard and assumed for years, but this is what the Word says.

"Oh, you're trying to diminish Jesus."

Not at all. I am not diminishing anything Jesus did. He is the forerunner. He is the one who did it, but He also passed the baton to us. He won the victory. Now we are supposed to take it, run with it, and bring it to its full conclusion.

In Genesis 3:15, God declared enmity between Eve's seed and the devil's seed. *Enmity* means to hate as one of an opposite tribe or nation. God was describing two kingdoms coming into conflict, warring against each other. Out of mankind He was going to bring forth a tribe of people, a kingdom, that was going to have enmity with the devil's tribe, his kingdom.

I have used many different Bible studies and resources to study this passage in Genesis 3. Every single source I found pointed me toward a specific cross-reference—Revelation 12:17. That verse says, "Then the dragon was enraged at the woman and went off to wage war against the rest of her offspring—those who keep God's commands and hold fast their testimony about Jesus." The word *offspring* there is the Greek equivalent of the Hebrew word in Genesis 3:15.

There is a war going on. But through the picture of Joshua, Jesus is telling us, "I won it! I triumphed over the enemy at the cross. I disarmed him. I made a public spectacle of him. Now, *you* come. *You* put *your* foot on his head."

This is the truth, and it is a truth we need to establish in our hearts and minds. Most of us don't live our lives like Jesus has given us victory and authority over the enemy. This is not theological speculation, up in the clouds. What you believe about Christ's victory and your part in it affects how you live your day-to-day life. If you truly get a hold of this truth, it will change the way you walk, and it will change the way you war.

The New Testament confirms this truth. Romans 16:20 says, "The God of peace will soon crush Satan under your feet." Whose feet will Satan soon be crushed under? Your feet. Not Jesus's feet. Jesus did crush Satan under His feet, but now He has given us the opportunity to do the same.

The King James Version says, "The God of peace shall bruise Satan under your feet." There is a problem with that translation of this verse. It's not strong enough. The Greek word translated as "crush" or "bruise" is the word *suntribó*, which means "to crush repeatedly." Not a one-time gotcha, but a continual crushing. People in New Testament times used this word to describe the crushing of grapes. In those days, they put the grapes in a vat, climbed into the vat, then stepped and stomped and crushed them over and over until all the juices had run out. That is a picture of what Jesus did to the devil and what we are called to do now.

Romans 16:20 also says that God will "*soon* crush Satan under your feet" (italics added). That is a bit of a mistranslation caused by a play on words. The word translated as "soon" is the Greek word *tachos*. In this case, *tachos* has much less to do with time and a lot more to do with marching. It means "to take short, pounding steps." We will crush Satan under our feet with short, pounding steps.

*Tachos* is what happened when the Roman army marched into a town. Can you imagine thousands of soldiers marching on a stone street? Boom, boom, boom. The people of the town did not need a radio report. Nobody sounded a siren. They knew what was happening. The whole place would have been shaking from the pounding, marching boots.

That is what God was saying, the picture He was trying to give us. We are going to take short, pounding, marching, repeated steps, crushing Satan underneath our feet. We are not talking about popping him a good one. We are not talking about backhanding him once and walking off. Crush him. Stomp on him over and over and over again. *Suntribó* him.

"Well, that's true for the pastor. That's true for the real, special saints of God."

No, that is true for you, beloved. It is so much easier to believe this for other people, but you absolutely must believe it for yourself. If you are in Christ Jesus, then you are going to crush Satan under your feet. That is part of your inheritance. That is part of who you are.

In Luke 10:18, Jesus tells his disciples, "I saw Satan fall like lightning from heaven. I have given you authority to trample on snakes and scorpions and to overcome all the power of the enemy; nothing will harm you."

"Myles, you don't really believe Jesus was talking to us, do you? Come on. That was just for the seventy-two disciples He was speaking to. That was specific to them. Besides, all that stuff ended in the first century. It died out with the apostles."

No, it didn't. Jesus was talking to His disciples, but this message is meant for us as well.

The word translated as "trample" in that verse is the Greek word *padeo*, which literally means "to march on or trample underfoot." Jesus has given us the authority to trample the devil underfoot. We have the power to march on his kingdom. Are you taking that authority? Are you using that power?

"Amen. Praise God. Hallelujah. Thank you, Jesus. Isn't that good? I have never seen that in the Word before."

You can say and think stuff like that all you want, it is not going to change your life. Get this. Believe it is true for you. Choose to possess it.

Jesus did not give you this authority so you could put it on a shelf somewhere and admire it every now and then. "Ooh, isn't it nice that Jesus gave me that? It's getting kind of dusty, let me blow it off." He gave us the authority so we would use it. He wants us to walk forward with it.

The word translated here as "trample" is the same word Revelation 14:17–20 uses to describe Jesus trampling the enemy at the end of the age. The first verse of the "Battle Hymn of the Republic" was based on that passage of Scripture.

> Mine eyes have seen the glory of the coming of the Lord;
> He is trampling out the vintage where the grapes of wrath
> are stored;
> He hath loosed the fateful lightning of His terrible swift sword:
> His truth is marching on.[17]

God wants you to march forward. He wants you to take authority over, trample on, and crush anything that gets in the way of advancing His kingdom in your life, in the life of your family, in the life of your church, and in the life of your community.

James 4:7 says, "Submit yourselves, then, to God. Resist the devil, and he will flee from you." The word *flee* means to run as if in terror. When you resist the devil the way God tells you to resist him, he will not back away from you slowly and carefully. He will flee from you as if in terror.

"You know, I just fought off the devil all week. It was battle after battle."

If you are a born-again Christian under continual attack from the enemy, something is wrong. Most likely you have one of two problems in your life. First, you do not know or are not taking the authority Jesus gave you. Do you know who you are in Christ? Is that identity firmly established in your heart and mind? Do you exercise that authority daily? If you can answer yes to these questions, the enemy should be running from you, and you might want to take a look at the second problem.

Second, you are not submitted to God. This problem comes from the first part of James 4:7. Resisting the enemy without submitting to God is like swatting flies with the window open—you can spend all day doing it without really accomplishing anything. Why don't you just close the window? Why don't you get rid of the sin in your life that is allowing the enemy constant entry?

Part of the word translated as "resist" in this verse (*anthistémi*) is the word we get "histamine" from. Our bodies produce histamine when they detect the presence of an outside agent like bacteria or an allergen. It is part of the immune response, increasing circulation and triggering the production and secretion of several different fluids. That is why our noses run and our eyes water when we get sick or our allergies flare up, and it is why we take medicines called antihistamines to combat those symptoms. Histamine defends our bodies from invaders by trying to flush them out.

That is part of the picture God is giving us in this verse. Resist the devil. When he comes in and invades your turf, flush him out like the outside agent he is.

James 4:7 was written in the present continuous tense of the Greek language. That means we are not talking about doing something just once. When you resist the enemy and he flees, do not expect him to stay gone for the rest of your life. He will come back. But if you keep coming against him, he will keep fleeing. Resist the devil every time he comes at you.

Resisting the devil is especially important if you are the head of your household. God has given you, fathers and single mothers, the responsibility to resist the devil for more than just yourself. When the enemy invades your home and comes against the members of your household, stand for them. "Hey! You're not coming into my house. Get out."

Do you have rebellious teenagers? Resist that influence of the enemy. Start declaring, "Get out of here, rebellion. You're not coming into my house." Come against it in prayer. Pray over your teenagers' rooms when they are gone to school. Pray over their clothes. Pray over whatever you can to resist the devil's kingdom in your house.

If you have young children in your house, it is not enough to just pray over them. You are also required and called by God to do the hard, dirty-fingernail work of child training.

In all of this, we are not called to come against flesh and blood. In fact, the Bible specifically warns us that "our struggle is not against flesh and blood" (Eph. 6:12). Don't try to take authority over anybody else's flesh. But that does not stop you from taking authority over the enemy coming against somebody else.

Is every headache from the devil? No, I am not saying that. But headaches are a part of his kingdom. I guarantee you they are not a part of God's. Resist them. Stand against them.

Sometimes people want to know how I pray when someone needs healing. What if it isn't God's will to heal at that moment? I always handle situations like that in the same way. Unless God tells me to stop, I'm going for it. I think that is very much in line with God's heart. I am going to pray for healing. I am going to do everything I can to bring the Kingdom. Unless the Holy Spirit says, "Whoa! Hold on," I am going to battle.

Most Christians spend their lives waiting for God to tell them to giddyup and go. We need to be like Paul. He wanted to spread the gospel in Bithynia. He strained and kept trying to go, but the Holy Spirit held him back. That is what biblical Christianity looks like. We need to go for it unless God says, "Uh-uh. There's an issue here. Slow down. Back up. Don't go there."

Years ago, before I understood the truth in this chapter, I prayed for people like this: "God, please heal this person. He's feeling bad. Would you please heal him?" One time I was praying for someone just like that when the Holy Spirit told me, clear as a bell, *Why are you asking Me to do this? I gave that authority to you. You do it.*

Most of us pray wimpy prayers. And we wonder why so few are touched or healed. We pray, "Oh Jesus, please take authority—"

He answers, "Hey! I gave the authority to you!"

Jesus already handed off the ball. We need to take the authority He has given us. We need to pray boldly, knowing who we are in Christ.

This is not me hung up on myself. I am under no delusions of who I am. Apart from Christ, I know very well who I am—nobody. But I also know what the Word says about who I am in Christ. I know the authority He has given to me.

If we are going to be the people God has called us to be and do the things He has called us to do, then we have to understand these things. If we are going to possess the inheritance given to us by God, then we have to put our feet on the neck of the enemy. We belong in that position. The devil belongs under our feet. If you don't like that, then your liker is broken.

The truth is a lot of people in the Church do not like this. They reject the truth because they believe this "resist the devil" stuff is unnecessary. They believe Christians just need to get their acts together and get their character right. They live very passive lives and walk in very passive forms of Christianity because they have been deceived by false teaching and the enemy.

"Oh, I'm not into all that spiritual warfare stuff. I've seen all those Charismatic squirrels running around and trying to blast demons all the time. Thank God I'm not out of balance like they are."

Guess what. You are out of balance. The "Charismatic squirrels" may not have it right, but you are in the ditch as well—just on the other side of the road.

Character is extremely important. I do not deny that. But this is not either-or. This is both-and. We need to build solid character *and* resist the enemy spiritually. You don't have to throw character and holiness out the window to engage in spiritual warfare and resist the devil. Add resisting the enemy to the godliness and character you already have.

Understand this: spiritual warfare will never be the emphasis or focal point of Grace Ministries International or any church body associated with it. If you are afraid of that, get rid of that fear. God did not give you a spirit of fear, so it is coming from the enemy, designed to keep you from entering into the battle. Jesus will always be the center of what we do, not spiritual warfare.

But, as a church, we also understand there are times and seasons when Jesus comes as a mighty warrior. That shouldn't surprise us. It is all over the Word. It is who He declares Himself to be many times. When He comes as a warring spirit, we will recognize Him and join Him in what He is doing.

How about you? Will you recognize Him when He comes into your life as a man of war? Sometimes we get so locked into one mindset the only time we recognize Jesus is when He comes in lamb-like mode. Soft and gentle. Sweet and easy. If the worship leader would just play those soft, sweet songs, then we could feel the presence of the Lord.

If that is the only way you recognize Jesus, then you have built a box around yourself. Rip it apart. Throw it away. Expand your vision and your understanding of who Jesus is. Many times He comes like a mighty warrior in our midst.

Does that mean the devil runs from us only when we shout? No. Does that mean the devil fears only warfare songs? No. In 2 Chronicles 20, God defeats a vast army of enemies for the Israelites while they do nothing but sing and worship. They were not singing songs of warfare. "Oh, let's go bash the devil's head in!" What were they singing? "Give thanks to the LORD, for his love endures forever" (20:21). They were just singing songs of praise to God, and God moved powerfully in spiritual warfare through their worship.

If you could see me when I am in prayer—for other people, for my family, for my church—I am sure you would think I am absolutely nuts. There are times when I waltz into God's presence and just enjoy Him. In those moments I worship Him, and He shows me his love. But there are other times when I march into His presence with short, pounding steps, trampling the enemy underfoot.

I try not to enter into prayer with any preconceptions about what the prayer time is going to be like. I come there to meet with God, and I let Him put within me what is on His heart.

God wants to well up the spirit of warfare within you. This is part of being a follower of Christ. This is part of leading your household. Stand and war over your life. Stand and war over your home. Resist the devil. Come against every part of his kingdom that encroaches upon your territory.

# Endnotes

1   J.R. Miller, *Unto the Hills: A Meditation on Psalm 121* (Editora Oxigênio, 2015).

2   Edward Young, quoted in Josiah Hotchkiss Gilbert, *Dictionary of Burning Words of Brilliant Writers* (New York: W. B. Ketcham, 1895), 206. Google Books. https://books.google.com/books?id=afENAAAAYAAJ.

3   A.W. Pink, *Spiritual Growth* (Reformed Church Publications, 2013), chap. 10, sec. 2. Google Books. https://www.google.com/books/edition/Spiritual_Growth

4   Roberts Liardon, *God's Generals: Smith Wigglesworth* (New Kensington, PA: Whitaker House, 2000). Google Books. https://books.google.com/books?id=RRD2BgAAQBAJ.

5   Jim Elliot, quoted in Kevin Halloran, "Jim Elliot's Journal Entry with 'He is No Fool…' Quote" https://www.kevinhalloran.net/jim-elliot-quote-he-is-no-fool/

6   Dr. Neil T. Anderson, *The Steps to Freedom in Christ: A Biblical Guide to Help You Resolve Personal and Spiritual Conflicts and Become a Fruitful Disciple of Jesus* (Bloomington, MN: Bethany House Publishers, 2017), loc. 696 of 938, Kindle.

7   Ibid., loc. 659 of 938

8   Ibid., loc. 659 of 938

9   Ibid., loc. 659 of 938

10  Ibid., loc. 659 of 938

[11]    Ibid., loc. 659 of 938

[12]    Ibid., loc. 677 of 938

[13]    Ibid., loc. 677 of 938

[14]    Ibid., loc. 659 of 938

[15]    Doris Day, vocalist, "Que Sera, Sera (Whatever Will Be, Will Be)," by Ray Evans and Jay Livingston, recorded May 21, 2956, *50's Classics*. DD's Collection, copyright 2011, Spotify.

[16]    Eugene Peterson, *A Long Obedience in the Same Direction: Discipleship in an Instant Society* (Downers Grove, IL: InterVarsity Press, 1980).

[17]    Julia Ward Howe, "The Battle Hymn of the Republic." *The Atlantic Monthly*, February 1862.